RECOVERING FROM GASLIGHTING

CONTENTS

INTRODUCTION

Do you ever feel like someone is trying to drive you crazy?

Are you in a relationship that makes you question everything about your life? Do you constantly feel confused and ungrounded, like you don't have a solid grasp on your reality? Does this person always tell you that you are remembering things incorrectly? Do you find yourself questioning your own perspective and judgement? Does this partner, parent, friend, or work colleague make you feel insecure and powerless? Are you unable to make simple decisions? Do you feel like everything that goes wrong in the relationship is your fault?

It may be that you love and trust this person, but you also know that something is wrong. You don't want to talk to anyone else about the relationship because you can't figure out how to explain what is happening. You're worried that the situation is unhealthy, but you can't pinpoint exactly why. More than anything, you don't know what to do. You are unhappy, anxious, frustrated, and lost, but you don't know how to escape this relationship.

If this describes what you are going through, it is likely that you are a victim of gaslighting.

Gaslighting is a form of emotional and psychological abuse. It is used as a tool to maintain power and control, and it includes various tactics of manipulation. Gaslighting attacks the core of someone's sense of self, and its goal is to make you doubt and question everything about your life and reality.

This abuse is incredibly effective at trapping its victims in toxic situations, but there *is* a way out. You can escape from this psychological and emotional minefield, and it is possible to recover from this experience.

Your Journey Out

This book aims to help you navigate the journey out of gaslighting, and it explores many different strategies for healing from this toxicity. It will provide you with extensive knowledge about the nature of gaslighting, and it will guide you on how to value, trust, and love yourself in the aftermath of emotional abuse.

To get you started on this journey, the first chapter of this book defines gaslighting in more detail. It breaks down this complicated topic in a way that can be easily recognized and understood. Chapter 2 then delves deeper into what this kind of abuse can look like, and it explores the various tools and tactics of manipulation used by gaslighters.

Chapter 3 will help you to understand how gaslighting is negatively impacting your life. It highlights the effects of this emotional and psychological abuse on how you view the world, how you think about yourself, and how you behave.

With this solid theoretical understanding in place, this book will move on to more practical strategies for dealing with gaslighting. Chapter 4 outlines how to call out a gaslighter's behavior and how best to combat their abuse by setting healthy boundaries.

The next chapter will build on this foundation by emphasizing the importance of space and support. Chapter 5 helps you to escape the clutches of your abuser so that you can see the situation from a distance and with better perspective.

Chapter 6 continues this theme, and it walks you through the most important message of this book: The most effective way to stop gaslighting is to end your relationship with the gaslighter. This chapter contains essential information about how to leave an abusive situation safely and how to prevent yourself from being sucked back in.

Chapter 7 sets us firmly in the healing and recovery stage of the journey out of gaslighting. It deals with the detrimental impact of this abuse on your self-worth, and it will help you to let go of the relationship by reaffirming your value and identity and giving yourself closure.

Similarly, Chapter 8 is focused on counteracting gaslighting's negative impact on your confidence and self-esteem. It highlights how this abuse violates your trust in yourself, and explores how you can regain this personal faith and self-belief.

Recovering from gaslighting is also about taking care of yourself. As such, Chapter 9 is centered on how to undo the stress, depression, anxiety, and trauma of this abuse and how to find joy in your life again.

Finally, Chapter 10 adds to this by guiding you out of the loneliness and isolation caused by gaslighting. It will also help you to safeguard yourself going forward by outlining red flags and warning signs to avoid in future relationships.

Above all else, this book will help you to accept that you are a survivor of abuse and that you did nothing to deserve what happened to you. It will give you hope for a full recovery, and all you need to do to begin your journey out of gaslighting is to take the first step.

CHAPTER 1:

WHAT IS GASLIGHTING?

● ●

Gaslighting is a form of abuse, and understanding exactly how it works is the best way to begin to cope with your experience.

This chapter starts by defining gaslighting in order to explain the nature of this abuse. It looks at the different aspects of this behavior, and explores how gaslighting is used to trap a victim in a toxic relationship. The origins of the term "gaslight" will also be examined, along with the theory behind why some people choose to treat others in this way. Finally, this chapter will highlight the different situations in which gaslighting can occur as a way of emphasizing the unequal power dynamics at play.

A Type of Abuse

Gaslighting is classified is a type of psychological and emotional abuse. It involves deliberate and consistent attempts by a person to make someone else doubt their own memory, opinion, perception, and judgement. The end result is that a victim of gaslighting will begin to question their entire reality and even their own sanity.

Gaslighting most commonly occurs in abusive relationships, and it involves someone using specific manipulation tactics to get their victim to question everything about themselves and their lives. This behavior is characterized by an ongoing pattern of lying, belittling, and minimizing in order to bully, control, and abuse another person. A gaslighter will consciously feed their victim false information to create a distorted narrative, with the goal of breaking down a person's trust, confidence, and perspective.

Above all else, gaslighting is about control and power. It is a deliberate effort to dismantle someone's self-worth and attack the core of their identity so that they will be entirely dependent on their abuser. Gaslighting is about oppression, which is why it is also common on a broader, systemic scale. These tactics are used by those in power to discredit, confuse, and disempower people who are already vulnerable or subjugated.

Trapped in Toxicity

Just like other forms of emotional or psychological manipulation, gaslighting can be difficult to spot. The main reason for this is because it begins slowly and intensifies gradually over time. The incremental escalation of this kind of abuse is by design, and abusers are conscious of the timeline of their actions.

Specifically, there is often no explicit sign of abuse at the beginning of a relationship with a gaslighter. In fact, it is usually the exact opposite. People who engage in emotional abuse initially work very hard to gain the trust and love of their victims. They dive headfirst into the honeymoon phase of a relationship, and their manipulation takes time to become apparent.

But, once they have your commitment and faith, a gaslighter will slowly begin to turn the tables. They may start to suggest that you are not reliable. They will say that you are forgetful, and will try to tell you that you are not remembering things correctly. Their goal is eventually to convince you that you are irrational, overreacting, or literally going insane.

Over time, these tactics escalate, and victims of gaslighting lose perspective entirely. They become deeply entangled in the relationship, and begin to believe what the abuser is telling them. Victims start to think that maybe things are their fault, that they do deserve the treatment they are receiving, and that perhaps this behavior is normal. They may even go so far as to defend the abuser's actions to themselves and others.

Ultimately, people who experience gaslighting become increasingly confused about what is happening to them. They are filled with doubt and uncertainty, and their confidence and self-esteem decline exponentially. It can be difficult for them to make decisions or see things clearly, and their mental health will be seriously impacted in a negative way. Depression, anxiety, chronic stress, addiction issues, and PTSD symptoms are all common for victims of gaslighting.

But perhaps the most significant consequence of this abuse is the dependency it fosters within its victims. Gaslighting is an incredibly effective tactic for trapping someone in a toxic relationship. Victims reach a state of such extreme self-doubt and reliance that they cannot even consider the possibility of leaving their abuser, which was the goal of the gaslighter all along.

The Origin Story

Gaslighting is not a new phenomenon. People have been engaging in psychological and emotional abuse throughout history, but the term "gaslight" is relatively modern. It originates from the name of a 1938 play written by English novelist and playwright Patrick Hamilton. The term was then further entrenched in contemporary nomenclature when the story was made into an American film in 1944.

Gas Light is a play about a husband who deliberately tries to drive his own wife insane so that he can cover up several of his crimes. The husband disappears from their home regularly, and refuses to tell his wife where he is going and why, even though he can see that it makes her anxious. He capitalizes on her vulnerability, and tries to convince her that she is losing her mind so that she will not discover what he is doing.

In actuality, the husband is sneaking into the apartment above theirs in order to steal jewels left behind by a woman who used to live there. By doing so, he makes a lot of noise and turns on the lights upstairs, which dims the gas lamps in his own home. The wife notices these changes in her environment, but she is told by her husband that she is imagining things. The husband also moves her possessions around, and then he tells her she has misplaced them. He cuts her off from all of her friends, and pretends that he is concerned for her while actively deceiving and manipulating her.

An Accurate Portrayal

By the end of the play, the wife feels completely out of control. She is neurotic and unsure of her memory and reality. She believes that she is indeed crazy, and it is only help from an outsider that allows her to see the truth. The husband was responsible for his wife's spiral into self-doubt, and he purposefully deceived her for his own gain. He wanted to take advantage of her, and he used her trust in him to do so. His actions were deliberate and calculated, and his behavior was designed to maintain his own control and power over the situation.

This overarching theme of the story resonated with society and remained relevant long after the play ended its run and the subsequent film finished showing. As early as the 1960s, writers and commentators began to use the word "gaslight" as a colloquialism for the behavior displayed by the husband. The narrative had such a cultural impact that gaslighting became synonymous with manipulation and deception.

Since then, the term has been officially adopted by those in the mental health profession. The story was believed to be such an accurate portrayal of the tactics of emotional abuse and manipulation that psychologists adopted this label in their practice. The actions and consequences of the fictional tale, although dramatized for suspense and entertainment, are clearly representative of the nature of true gaslighting relationships.

Where reality differs is in the motives of a real-life gaslighter. Not every abuser needs to cover up a crime, so why do some people gaslight others?

Learned Behavior

Gaslighting is a learned behavior, and those who engage in it do so because they have witnessed it as an effective tactic. It is common for a gaslighter to have parents who engage(d) in this kind of emotional and psychological abuse, and they would have spent their childhood watching one caregiver gain advantage and control over the other through manipulation. As this person grows, they don't learn any other way of interacting with those around them, and they are not taught what a healthy relationship looks like. In short, they become incapable of acting in any other way.

In addition to these aspects of their early childhood environment, gaslighters tend to have personalities that are predisposed to this behavior. Gaslighting has been linked to mental health disorders like narcissism, psychopathy, borderline personality disorder, and antisocial personality disorder. These traits are often underpinned by an intense need for attention as well as a lack of empathy. Individuals who have this psychological makeup believe that they are entitled to getting what they want and that the needs of others are not important. They consider themselves superior, and cannot accept things that do not go their way.

No Excuse

It is this upbringing and these personal characteristics that lay the foundation for gaslighting, and as we have seen, this abuse is solely about power and control. Some people simply get a sort of warped enjoyment from being able to deceive and manipulate others. They both like and need to be in control of all interpersonal interactions, and they are not able to engage with others in an honest and healthy way.

Moreover, gaslighters get pleasure out of making their victims complicit in the abuse. This is not at all to say that victims are responsible for what has happened to them—rather, emotional abusers are extremely effective at gaining misguided trust and cooperation. This allows them to escape responsibility for what they have done.

It is possible for someone to engage in gaslighting without knowing it. The behavior goes back to the foundations of their early childhood development, and they might not be aware of why they enjoying wielding power over others. It is important to remember that they do still enjoy this control, and being unable to articulate or understand this part of themselves does not relieve them of wrongdoing. Ignorance and lack of self-awareness is not a valid excuse. There is no acceptable reason for using gaslighting or any other form of emotional abuse.

Imbalance of Power

The theory behind why some people gaslight others is supported by the different situations in which this abuse occurs. While anyone can engage in gaslighting, it is most often evident in situations and relationships involving unequal power dynamics. It is this imbalance of power—and an abuser's desperate need to maintain it—that underpins gaslighting behavior.

Romance on Fire

Gaslighting is most commonly found in intimate and romantic relationships that are already one-sided or abusive in some way. The dominant or controlling partner uses gaslighting to isolate the other person and undermine their confidence.

The goal is to make this person easier to control because a gaslighter has to have things their way. They don't want their partner questioning, challenging, or trying to leave them. They definitely do not want their partner telling others about the behavior or getting a different perspective on their treatment from an outsider. So, to maintain the upper hand, gaslighters lie, bully, and manipulate the person they are supposed to love and care for.

This behavior is on brand for a narcissist who cannot see anyone else's perspective and cannot even begin to fathom that they might be the one at fault. Similarly, a person with psychopathic tendencies will not even care that they might be hurting a loved one with their behavior. Even gaslighters with borderline personality disorder may not be able to change their ways. Given the very nature of their psychology, their re-lationships are characterized by instability and intensity. They are not able to attach securely to others, and they feel unsafe when people get too close. As such, they will do anything to stay in control—just like all gaslighters.

Gaslighting exists outside of romantic partnerships, and while it can look slightly different in each case, the core of the behavior is consistent.

Keeping It in the Family

Gaslighting also occurs frequently between a parent and a child. Caregivers will undermine their charges in order to make them more obedient and easier to control. For example, when children are crying or in distress, an impatient and insensitive parent may try to shame them as a way of getting them to be quiet. They would say something like, "You're being too sensi-tive, and you're making a scene."

At the center of this behavior is an unwillingness to take the child's needs seriously, and denying the importance of someone's experience is a key element of gaslighting. This way of engaging with a child is common with narcissistic and detached parents, and as the child continues to grow, they are repeatedly manipulated into believing that their thoughts and feelings don't matter. The result is the same as with all gaslighting victims—the child becomes anxious, confused, and inse-cure. Moreover, since this abuse was so integral to their forma-tive years, these consequences often define their adulthood.

In much the same way, gaslighting can occur in any relation-ship between family members as well as in manipulative and toxic friendships. The tricky thing about gaslighters is that they can be very charming and charismatic people. They easily pull others into their orbit, and have no trouble getting loved ones to fall for their tactics.

Once a gaslighter has you hooked, it is very difficult to get them out of your head. They are good at making you want to be close to them, and making it seem like a privilege to re-ceive their attention. However, they will take advantage of this existing relationship and use it to manipulate you further. To make matters worse, because the gaslighter is a trusted family member or friend, it is hard to spot their behavior for what it is—abuse.

A Societal Scale

Unfortunately, gaslighting exists beyond close and personal relationships with those you love. In fact, this form of abuse is present at almost every level of society, and it permeates a variety of institutions.

Gaslighting can occur in companies or organizations when the people in charge use manipulation and psychological abuse to control those they have power over. This type of gas-lighting is often derived from existing economic, social, and gender inequalities. For example, management can try to dis-credit any workers who want to stand up for their own rights by labelling them as greedy or only in it for the money. Or, wom-en reporting problems or suggesting change can be silenced and dismissed by people who characterize them as irrational or unstable. The persecution of whistleblowers is another clear example of this type of gaslighting, as these individuals are regularly framed as incompetent traitors who are trying to take the company down for their own personal gain.

In addition to the workplace, one can also encounter gaslighting in other areas of life. Medical gaslighting is a newly acknowledged phenomenon, and it refers to a situation in which a medical professional dismisses someone's health concerns or symptoms as imagined or exaggerated. This is particularly common with patients who are women or people of color, especially when they report pain and discomfort. Doctors downplay or ignore their experience, and do not trust that the patients correctly understand their reality. They tell these patients that it is all in their head, and label them as hypochondriacs.

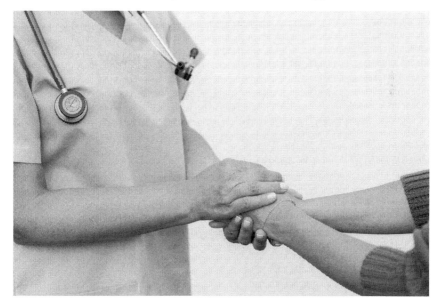

On the topic of racism, racial gaslighting is also prevalent in much of modern society. Racial gaslighting is when the tactics of this form of abuse are applied to a whole ethnic or racial group. The goal is often to discredit this entire sector of society as not worth listening to. It can be seen most clearly when activists of color are advocating for change, and those in power dismiss them as irrational or dangerous. A frequent technique of racial gaslighting is to pretend that racism doesn't exist and to argue that people are making a big deal out of nothing.

Similarly, gaslighting in the political sphere is an attempt by the powers that be to convince the public that they are not really experiencing the difficulties or hardships that they know to be true. Political gaslighting primarily involves the manipulation of information as a means of controlling the people. A political party or government will use propaganda, censorship, and denial to make its supporters doubt their reality. Moreover, politicians will downplay their actions and avoid responsibility in an effort to stay in power. They will discredit their opposition as unstable and threatening, and will try to draw attention away from their own failings and unfulfilled promises.

Going Forward

Having come to the end of this first chapter, it should be clear that gaslighting is a complex and delicate topic. This behavior is insidious and manipulative, and it has toxic consequences for victims and survivors. Moreover, this abuse can rear its ugly head in a variety of situations and relationships.

While this can be overwhelming to contemplate, you can take comfort in the fact that you now have a much better understanding of how gaslighting functions as a form of abuse. You have learned where the term comes from and how the behavior is rooted in power imbalances. You can be wary of gaslighting when operating in different areas of society, and you should be able to spot those who are trying to manipulate and control you. To help you with this, the next chapter will look more closely at the various tools that gaslighters use to carry out their abuse.

CHAPTER 2:

TACTICS AND TOOLS OF MANIPULATION

There are several specific techniques that gaslighters use to maintain their power and control over others. Being able to spot these strategies can help you understand what is happening to you and enable you to identify abusive and manipulative behavior.

This chapter highlights the many tools of gaslighters, and it starts by exploring lying as the foundational tactic used by these manipulators. It will also examine how gaslighters get their victims to question everything about their reality by rewriting history, withholding, and denying. Techniques like diverting, trivializing, and stereotyping will also be discussed to show how emotional abusers are experts at changing the subject when confronted or challenged. Finally, this chapter looks at countering, discrediting, and love bombing to explain how gaslighters make everything seem as though it is your fault.

The Foundation of Gaslighting

The cornerstone of gaslighting abuse is lying.

Gaslighters are usually habitual and even pathological liars. They blatantly misrepresent the truth, and seem to concoct stories and details out of thin air. Gaslighters have little hesitation or remorse when lying, and they rarely back down from their version of events. Even when called out or confronted with explicit evidence that proves them wrong, they are compulsively stubborn in their dishonesty.

Since you may not know the truth that you are trying to uncover, it is easier to spot lying by how a gaslighter responds to your attempts to engage with them. They may regularly say things like, "That never happened," "I never did that," or "I did not say that." Speaking in absolutes like these is almost always a sure sign that you are being lied to.

In addition to these outright falsehoods, gaslighters will frequently distort the truth in little ways. This entails an abundance of white lies and lies of omission, and gaslighters are careful in what they choose to tell you. Often, a gaslighter will deliberately leave out information in order to confuse and manipulate you. It is easier to make you think you are wrong when you don't have the full story.

Blurring the Truth

As the volume of misinformation grows, it becomes increasingly difficult for victims of a lying gaslighter to see the truth. This is intentional on the part of the abuser, and gaslighters are effective at distorting the truth primarily because they get so much practice. They can be very convincing in their lies, and over time, victims become too confused and exhausted to do anything except second-guess and doubt themselves.

It is also common for gaslighters to turn the tables and accuse the victim of being the liar. They will say things like "You're making that up" to get the attention off of their own dishonesty. All of these efforts further blur the lines between truth and fiction, and victims can get lost in the lack of clarity.

Question Everything

Gaslighters also use other tactics to get their victims to doubt reality. Their goal is to make you question what you think, what you remember, and even what you feel, and they have different tools for distorting your perception in this way.

Rewriting History

Building on the foundation of lies and misinformation, gaslighters tend to rewrite history to make their victim question their own memory and recollection.

Gaslighters always seems to have their own version of what happened, and they like to rewrite the past in a way that paints them in a better light. A gaslighter is seemingly never the "bad guy" in their own retelling of events, and they present an alternate reality as a way of trying to manipulate your perception. The intention is to create confusion and doubt and to place the power of knowledge and information in their own hands.

An effective way of spotting this tactic is to be critical of what the gaslighter is telling you. They are deliberately trying to get you to doubt your memory, so rely instead on your critical thinking. A gaslighter's story will never make complete sense and it won't quite match up with what other people say happened. While there are usually two sides to every story, if every retelling by the gaslighting makes them out to be the hero or victim—but never the villain—then it is likely that they are trying to rewrite what actually happened.

Withholding

Gaslighters also regularly use withholding as a tactic to get you to question what is happening around you. Withholding is when an abuser refuses to engage with their victim by not listening to the conversation or pretending not to know what they are talking about.

When confronted or challenged, a gaslighter will use withholding to become a brick wall. They will not acknowledge what the other person is trying to communicate, and they will not react to what is happening. Instead, they will usually sit silently and show no emotion while their victim becomes increasingly frustrated and distressed. What's worse, gaslighters can use this situation to make themselves into a victim. They will take advantage of how upset you are, and accuse you of attacking them. You become the villain, and they are the martyr who passively accepts your anger.

Withholding is also more overt when a gaslighter is explicit in their dismissal of a victim. They can say things like "I don't want to hear about this now" and "You just want to confuse me." They are essentially accusing *you* of trying to gaslight *them*, and this psychological torture can warp your entire perspective of what is really going on.

If you have been on the receiving end of this tactic, you will know how devastating it can be. You are trying to make things work and resolve an issue, and the gaslighter is refusing to recognize this reality. Their goal is to escape responsibility for what they have done, and you become so exhausted by the effort of getting them to engage that eventually you are forced to let it go.

By withholding their thoughts and emotions from you, the gaslighter can convince you that nothing is wrong. They can get you to question your perception of the situation by pretending like nothing happened, and in the end, they pull you into this playacting. There is no possibility of resolution, reconciliation, or closure on the issue, so you too must pretend as though nothing has happened.

Denying

A similar technique of dismissing a victim is when gaslighters deny anything and everything. This goes back to the foundational pillar of gaslighting, and an abuser's denial of events and actions is another way in which they are trying to lie to you. They will pretend to forget what has happened, and they will swear that they never said or did the things you are talking about.

This is in an effort to absolve themselves of responsibility, and it is underpinned by their refusal to take accountability for their actions. Emotional abusers are notorious for believing that they have done nothing wrong, and denying wrongdoing is an incredibly common variation of this tactic. Gaslighters will pretend like they don't know that they have hurt you, and will never acknowledge that they should have behaved differently.

They will also frequently deny promises that they have made. "I don't know what you're talking about" is something they'll say on a regular basis to manipulate you into thinking that you are misremembering the past. They will try to get you to believe that you misunderstood or misheard them so that they don't have to take the blame for not following through.

This technique leaves its victim feeling confused, unseen, and unheard. They begin to doubt what really happened, and the lack of closure and acknowledgement makes it difficult to cope with these feelings.

Let's Change the Subject

There is another set of techniques that gaslighters use to manipulate their victims and avoid responsibility. These tools are designed to change the subject away from the gaslighter's behavior in order to prevent you from seeing the truth of the abuse. The goal is to minimize the seriousness of the gaslighter's actions and to convince you that there is nothing to be concerned about.

Diverting

Diverting is when a gaslighter deliberately changes the topic of conversation when you try to call out their behavior or engage with them on an issue that is important to you. The most common diversionary tactic is to downplay the situation and to question the victim's credibility in raising the issue.

"You're imagining things," "You shouldn't believe everything that so-and-so tells you," and "This is just another silly idea of yours." These are all diverting and distracting statements, and they are designed to shift your attention away from the issue at hand. Diverting allows the gaslighter to avoid having to respond to what you are saying, and this dismissal makes you doubt whether what you had to say is really all that important. After all, if they don't feel the need to address it, then why are you taking things so seriously?

Diverting is effective because it convinces victims that they are making a big deal out of nothing or are focusing their attention on the wrong thing. The result is that they let the issue slide, and the gaslighter gets away with their manipulation.

Trivializing

Another really significant way in which gaslighters downplay their actions is by minimizing the effects their behavior has on a victim. Gaslighters do this by trivializing the victim's emotions and intentionally belittling and disregarding what they might be feeling.

It is in this technique that the meanness and bullying of gaslighting is most apparent. Gaslighters will explicitly insult victims and demean their needs to get the victim to believe that they are not important. The goal of trivializing is to convince the victim that they are overreacting and irrational. A gaslighter wants you to think that your feelings aren't real and that your needs don't matter so that you will continue to put them first. They want to be the powerful one in the relationship, and they want things done their way. The best way to achieve this is to get you to ignore your own discomfort, pain, and abuse.

Trivializing usually happens when you try to express your feelings to a gaslighter. You may have legitimate concerns and valid emotions that you want to discuss, but the response of the gaslighter will be something along the lines of "You're too sensitive" or "Why do you always have to get worked up over little things?". They are essentially telling you that what you are feeling is wrong and irrelevant, and this can be very shaming, invalidating, and isolating.

Victims of trivializing genuinely come to believe that their opinions and needs don't matter, and so they stop expressing them. Moreover, they too begin to question the validity of their feelings, and it becomes impossible to process the emotions that they—and their abuser—refuse to acknowledge as real.

Stereotyping

A final strategy that gaslighters use to change the subject when confronted is stereotyping. This is when an abuser deliberately applies stereotypes related to race, age, gender, sexuality, or nationality as a way of manipulating their victims.

As we saw in Chapter 1, this kind of tool is most common in institutional, racial, and political forms of gaslighting. Existing socio-economic, racial, and gender inequalities are exploited by those in power to control others, and stereotypes are used to dismiss and disempower entire groups and categories of society.

Stereotyping can also be used by gaslighters in intimate re-lationships, and abusers are adept at using existing prejudices to control their victims. These can be subtle implications like trying to convince a younger partner that their needs are im-mature and that they don't have enough experience to know what a healthy relationship looks like. Gaslighters can also be more direct with this stereotyping tactic: "No one believes women who say they have been abused."

It's Not Me, It's You

The final category of tools and tactics that gaslighters use to manipulate others is all about shifting blame to the victim.

These abusers are experts at victim shaming, and they will deliberately try to make victims believe that they are complicit in their own abuse.

Countering

Countering is a technique whereby gaslighters question a victim's memory and recollections to make them think that they are at fault. This manipulation creates doubt and confusion, but it also twists a person's perception of reality to such an extent that they truly believe they must be wrong.

When countering, gaslighters will say things like "You're forgetting what really happened" and "Are you sure about that?". The effectiveness of this tool is that it allows an abuser to turn every conversation on its head. You may start off by being certain of something that happened and eager to call the person out on it, but once they start countering what you remember, it can be difficult to stay confident. All of a sudden, they've made it seem like you are at fault and wrong, and you begin to question whether the gaslighter is right.

Countering is one of the most common techniques used by gaslighters. Moreover, it is a strategy that can initially appear harmless but then escalate to a dangerous degree. For example, gaslighters may first engage in countering in a very lighthearted manner. They may jokingly suggest that you have a bad memory or can never get your facts straight. But, over time, gaslighters will repeatedly tell you that you are unreliable and cannot be trusted.

Eventually, you will start to believe this about yourself, and begin to rely on your abuser to define your memory and reality. This makes you extremely vulnerable to manipulation, and it also robs you of your agency and power in the relationship.

Discrediting

As with stereotyping, we touched briefly on discrediting in Chapter 1. This is a gaslighting technique frequently used by the powerful across various sectors of society. Unfortunately, discrediting is equally insidious, manipulative, and abusive on an interpersonal and intimate level.

Gaslighters often gossip and spread rumors about their victims. They will approach their friends, family, and loved ones, and pretend to be concerned about the person while actually trying to get others to believe they are unstable, lying, or delusional. The goal of discrediting is to make the victim seem like the problem and to ensure that no one will believe them if they come forward about their abuse. It is an effort to isolate someone from those they care about so that they will not tell anyone the truth.

Discrediting is very effective because a gaslighter will use the same manipulative tactics across many relationships. They can turn someone's loved ones against them by lying and distorting the truth. A gaslighter will tell part of the story, exaggerate details, and play the hero or victim. At the core of this tactic is a gaslighter's ability to present one face to the world and another to their victim. They will intentionally convince others to take their side, and will be very concerned about whether people perceive them in a good light.

Discrediting is also done the other way around, and a gas-lighter will lie to their victim and say that their loved ones are talking badly about them. The gaslighter's aim is to manipulate their victim into thinking they have no support and that they would have nowhere to go if they wanted to leave.

Love Bombing

Gaslighters are also two-faced in other ways when trying to maintain control over their victims, and the best example of this is their use of love bombing.

Love bombing is when emotional abusers use love and kind-ness as weapons and tools of manipulation. For example, an abuser will be overly compassionate and concerned for some-one as a way of resolving conflicting and avoiding responsi-bility. Instead of addressing the issue raised, gaslighters will bombard their partners with compliments and love to soothe over and dismiss their concerns. They may say something like, "You know that I love you more than anything. I would never hurt you."

The goal of love bombing is to exploit your care, consider-ation, and empathy. The gaslighter wants you to focus on their apparent vulnerability and love for you and to forget about how their behavior has really hurt you. This manipulation is ef-fective because a lot of what an abuser says when they love bomb is exactly what you want to hear—and they know it.

When you are stuck in an abusive relationship, you are very unused to explicit love and flattery. Love bombing catches you off guard, distracts you, and makes you more amenable to let-ting things go. You begin to think that they will finally give you what you need and treat you how you deserve. You get caught up by all the lovely things they are saying, and you forget why you were upset in the first place, even though the issue has not been addressed at all.

It is also a very common tactic at the beginning of the re-lationship, and gaslighters double down on love bombing in the honeymoon phase. They will compliment and confide in you, and will use disclosure and praise to establish trust far too quickly. This moves things along rapidly, and before you know it, you are wrapped up in their world, and your deep trust in them makes you easier to manipulate.

The hard truth is that love bombing is not authentic intimacy—it is simply manipulation. The gaslighter is telling you what you want to hear so that you will love and forgive them.

CHAPTER 3:

RECOGNIZING THE SIGNS

As we saw in the previous chapter, gaslighters have many different tools and tactics for maintaining power and control. These strategies can be subtle and insidious, and the first step to recovering from gaslighting is being able to recognize this behavior for what it is. Moreover, you need to have a clear idea of why gaslighting is so dangerous, and you have to be aware of the various consequences of this abuse.

This chapter looks more closely at the impact of gaslighting on its victims. It explains how this abuse targets a person's core sense of self and uses gradual and repeated efforts to undermine their identity. Ultimately, gaslighting abuse can detrimentally affect every aspect of its victim—their perception of reality, the beliefs and views they hold of themselves, and the way they behave.

Dangerous Dynamics

Gaslighting is dangerous because the unique dynamics of this abuse are so effective in breaking down a person's agency and independence. This behavior targets the very core of a victim's sense of self to make them powerless and dependent. It creates and then deliberately exploits trust and intimacy in order to solidify the abuser's control. Finally, gaslighting uses repetition to reinforce the consequences of its manipulation.

Undermining the Self

Gaslighting attacks a person's entire sense of self and identity. Its aim is to get the victim to feel uncertain and unstable about who they are and what they are experiencing.

The different tactics of gaslighting can leave a person confused and ungrounded. They start to believe that they can't trust their own memory or judgement. Victims will second-guess their recollections, and become doubtful about their ability to understand what is going on around them. They'll begin to think of themselves as unreliable and incompetent.

In this way, gaslighting causes a victim to reshape their identity according to what their abuser is saying and doing to them. They are being intentionally manipulated into thinking they are not good enough and can't do anything right. Their abuser is deliberately getting them to question their past and present experiences, and ultimately, in order for the victim's mind to cope with the confusion and contradiction, it complies.

This is the danger of psychological abuse: It compels a person to abandon themself in favor of someone else's version of reality. It forces them to depend on their abuser to make sense of the world for them, and the end result is devastating for a victim's mental health. Depression, anxiety, PTSD, addiction, and suicidal ideation are all possible outcomes of gaslighting abuse.

Exploiting Trust

Another insidious feature of gaslighting is how hard abusers work to gain a victim's trust and love only to then exploit this intimacy for their own gain.

Gaslighting begins slowly and tactfully. Abusers focus on love bombing in the honeymoon phase, and only gradually begin to lie and deceive. They are cautious in how quickly they try to break down their victim, but over time, gaslighters double down on their efforts. They will use tools like countering and diverting if their victim starts to resist or rebel, and the abuse eventually escalates to discrediting and trivializing. In the end, the slow progression of manipulation creates a vicelike grip of control over the victim.

By appearing harmless and loving at first, an emotional abuser can establish deep trust and intimacy. They use a longer timeline to strengthen this foundation so that their victim grows increasingly attached to them. This means that by the time the abuse is more explicit the victim is already tangled up with their abuser in a mess of love and dependency.

Ultimately, it seems impossible for a victim to leave. Moreover, they can't even begin to fathom when things went wrong. They don't understand how things got so bad, and can't pinpoint when the other person's behavior crossed the line. It all happened so gradually and insidiously, which is why it was so effective. Above all, gaslighting works because victims learn and grow to trust their abusers.

Reinforcing With Repetition

Finally, true gaslighting is defined by repetition. This behavior is so successful because it is repeated consistently and regularly across situations.

Gaslighters don't simply try to manipulate you once. They don't just lie every now and then, and their controlling nature won't show up in some instances but not others. Gaslighting abuse is subtle and hard to spot, but it is persistent and always present. Manipulation is a compulsive and enduring pattern for these individuals, and even if you can't see it right away, everything they do is a calculated effort to control you.

Furthermore, the repetition of these efforts is what reinforces their effectiveness. When you are constantly told the same thing or treated in the same way, you can become desensitized to it. The more a gaslighter abuses you, the more "normal" the behavior feels and the less resistance you put up. They use a variety of different tools for the same purpose of achieving and maintaining power, and having to fight a battle of several fronts means an inevitable defeat for the victim.

The First Step

When done right, gaslighting is more dangerous and effective than people think, and anyone is susceptible to this kind of abuse. Gaslighting works best when it is subtle and hard to detect, and it exerts the most control and power when victims are unaware of what is going on. As such, recognizing its dynamics and consequences is the best way to counteract this insidious manipulation. Acknowledging gaslighting behavior as abuse and understanding its impacts is the cornerstone of your healing journey.

You have already learned a wealth of information about the nature of gaslighting in this and previous chapters. But you can also focus on your own thoughts, feelings, and actions to see things more clearly. Because gaslighting is so gradual and well disguised, it is often more effectively recognized by the impact on the victim rather than the behavior of the abuser. So, you can begin your journey out of psychological abuse by looking closely at the consequences of gaslighting outlined below.

Importantly, you do not need to meet every single point as a requirement to conclude that you are a victim of gaslighting. Instead, try to focus on the broad and overall impact of the toxic relationship. How has it affected your confidence in yourself and your reality? Has it changed how you see yourself as a person? What is different about your behavior and the way(s) in which you relate to others?

Your Perception of Reality

A sure sign that you are a victim of gaslighting is constantly feeling ungrounded and unstable.

Gaslighting will make you feel like you don't have a solid grasp on your own life and experiences. You can't trust that what you remember or feel is real, and you are always trying to convince yourself that everything is okay and the treatment you are receiving is normal. You've lost perspective on what a healthy relationship is supposed to look like and how love is supposed to make you feel.

Questions

Another consequence of gaslighting is that you ask a lot of questions. It may seem like everything you say is a question: "Did that really happen," "When did I say that," or "Can you remind me about that?" You ask others about past events and experiences that you have lived through, and you aren't ever truly confident in the details of your recollections. You seem to have a vivid imagination, and you worry that you are exaggerating things and making a big deal out of something that really isn't that bad.

Confusion and Concern

Essentially, your life is defined by confusion, and you feel lost and uncertain all of the time. The gaslighter's behavior is especially confusing and frustrating to you. Like Dr. Jekyll and Mr. Hyde, the gaslighter seems like two completely different people, and you spend an extraordinary amount of time thinking about them. You are constantly trying to riddle out what they are thinking and why they act the way they do.

Moreover, you are overly concerned with what they want, and you don't know how to make them happy. It seems like you are always putting them first and letting them define who you are and what you do. Your entire life revolves around them, and you can't understand how things came to be this way. When did you let yourself become so unimportant? How did you get so lost in this other person?

Impending Doom

Similarly, you just can't seem to understand why you aren't happier. You are sure that you have good things in your life and many reasons to be happy, but you know something is wrong. Deep down, you always feel off in some way, and it is too hard to explain exactly what is upsetting you.

You have a sense that things are going to go wrong and that something bad is going to happen. It feels as though there is a dark cloud over your head, and you have a feeling of impending doom. You are always on edge and hypervigilant, especially when you are around your abuser, and this further confuses and overwhelms you because you love and trust this person.

Beliefs About Yourself

You can also spot the impacts of gaslighting in the way in which you view yourself. You may start to wonder if there is something fundamentally wrong with you. You seem to have all of these problems and concerns with the relationship that the other person doesn't. It feels like you are always the one picking a fight or trying to make things work. So, maybe it is your fault? Maybe you are the problem?

Not Good Enough

Victims of gaslighting start to think that their expectations are unrealistic and irrational. You tell yourself that you are being too sensitive and that you shouldn't overreact so much. The gaslighter says that you can't take a joke and you need a thicker skin, and you begin to believe that they are right. You spend a lot of time criticizing yourself, repeating insults and negative self-talk, and reinforcing the idea that you need to be "better."

At the same time, you are constantly disappointed in yourself. You feel like you are never good enough, and you know that others must be disappointed in you too. Your confidence and self-esteem have declined drastically, and you find yourself feeling more insecure and vulnerable than ever before. You feel like you have failed somehow and have turned into a weak, inadequate, and unintelligent person. You are sure that you used to be more fun and relaxed. You know that you were once strong and confident, but now you feel like you've let yourself down.

Crazy

Ultimately, all of this self-doubt and dislike causes you to question your mental health. You wonder whether you might actually be going crazy, and think that maybe you need to get some help.

Over time, you lose sight of the fact that it is the gaslighter's behavior driving your confusion, and you can only see that there must be something wrong with you. You feel like a bad person, and believe that you are the one that needs to change.

Changes to Your Behavior

Additionally, you can look at how you behave with and relate to the gaslighter to see if you are a victim of this kind of abuse. The way you respond to those who question your relationship can also provide important clues.

Sorry, Sorry, Sorry

A common behavioral outcome of gaslighting is that you are always apologizing. It seems like you say sorry so often that it loses its meaning. Somehow, you are always the one apologizing and making amends, and the gaslighter is always the victim. They never apologize to you, and you are solely responsible for reconciling every issue, even when you did nothing wrong.

Moreover, you feel like you are always walking on eggshells around your abuser and you can never do anything right. You even find yourself apologizing for things that they have done. You use phrases like "I'm sorry I pushed you to do that," "I should have known better," and "It's actually my fault." Ultimately, you start to apologize for who you are, and you promise them that you will change and be better.

Another common behavior among victims of gaslighting is to defend the treatment they receive. You may find yourself telling others that it's not as bad as it seems or that your abuser hasn't really done anything wrong. You defend and support them, and you make excuses for them all of the time.

If someone questions your relationship, you tend to focus on what you have done and how you might be at fault. More often than not, you will explain away any toxic behavior by saying that you are just as bad or that the situation is complicated. You use this denial on yourself as well, and you tell yourself that other people don't know the full story and that they don't understand your relationship.

Staying Quiet

You try to avoid this discussion altogether. You become reluctant to talk about the relationship with your loved ones, and you withhold information so that you don't have to make excuses. It feels easier to lie and omit details than to try to explain what is really happening. You don't like feeling as though you have to justify why you are still in the relationship. Deep down, you know that it is unhealthy, but you are too overwhelmed, embarrassed, and confused to admit this or ask for help.

Instead, you avoid having to talk about it by isolating yourself from others. You withdraw from your other relationships, stop going out as much, and don't like to meet up with people who will ask about the situation. The loneliness and isolation makes you feel powerless and trapped, but you feel like you deserve it because it was your choice (right?). To feel better, you try to convince yourself that those people didn't really care about you anyway. You tell yourself that they don't support your relationship and probably think you're crazy.

In the same way that you are afraid to open up to others, you are fearful of speaking up to the gaslighter. It seems like you always say the wrong thing, and that every conversation turns into a fight. You don't like to express your emotions because you are worried that they will dismiss or ridicule you. It feels like it has been a very long time since you had an honest discussion, and you spend a lot of your time biting your tongue and staying silent.

You have learned that it is not worth it to speak your mind, and moreover, you are too uncertain about your life and past in any case. It makes you anxious and nervous to stand up to your abuser because you are worried that you might be remembering things incorrectly. You also know from experience that no matter what you say, they will try to twist your words and confuse you.

Giving up Control

In addition to feeling like you can't communicate properly anymore, gaslighting also makes you feel like you can't make decisions for yourself. You find that you have become a very indecisive and insecure person, and even little and everyday choices fill you with anxiety. The idea of making a mistake is terrifying, so you avoid decision-making altogether.

Worse still, you prefer to let the gaslighter choose for you. You believe that they know better and that you can't do anything right anyway. Over time, you find that you have put them in charge of every aspect of your life. It seems like they get to decide where you go, what you do, and who you talk to. You feel like you have no control over your life, but at the same time, you don't want this control back because you are convinced that you can't handle the responsibility.

Hope in Healing

If you can recognize that you exhibit some of these symptoms, you have already taken your first step toward healing.

Discovering that you relate to the consequences of gaslighting is difficult and scary. It can be daunting and upsetting to realize the extent to which this behavior has impacted your life and sense of self. But there is also a lot of hope in this knowledge. You can move forward with your eyes wide open. You are now equipped with the insight to escape toxicity, and you can begin to heal from this emotional and psychological abuse.

CHAPTER 4:

DEALING WITH A GASLIGHTER

● ●

By this point in the book, you should have a solid theoretical understanding of gaslighting—the nature of this abuse and the tools and tactics it entails. You should also be more aware of the impacts that this behavior can have on you and fully able to recognize this abuse and manipulation for what it is.

Now, it is time to put this knowledge into practical use when dealing with a gaslighter. This chapter is about how best to engage with someone who uses this form of emotional and psychological abuse. It begins by encouraging you to speak up about your experiences because this is the most effective way to acknowledge and confront the abuse. Above all else, the key to calling out a gaslighter is to remain confident in your own reality.

This chapter will also explore what not to do when dealing with an abuser, and the most important thing to remember is to be protective of your physical and emotional safety. Speaking up is your own choice, and you should always be mindful of the risks involved. In addition to confronting your abuser, you can focus on creating healthy boundaries, and this chapter will outline how best to do that.

Speaking Up

Gaslighting works because it undermines your confidence and self-esteem in a variety of different ways. This behavior confuses and manipulates you with misdirection, lies, criticism, and alternative realities. As such, it is not surprising that many people struggle to know how to respond to gaslighting techniques.

The key is not to allow yourself to be silenced. You have educated yourself on the tools and consequences of gaslighting, and you are able to recognize this behavior for what it is. Now, you need to work on speaking up when you experience it.

It's important not to be afraid of calling out or confronting a gaslighter about their behavior. This is the best way to acknowledge and address the abuse, and it helps to make yourself more aware of what is happening. Speaking up as a response to gaslighting works to counteract the main goal of this manipulation—making you believe that you are not experiencing or feeling something that you know to be real.

Calling out a gaslighter indicates to them that their tactics are not effective. It is a means of saying that you know what they are up to and that you are fully aware that they are trying to manipulate and control you. Over time, this will incentivize your abuser to leave you alone. Moreover, confronting a gaslighter about their behavior is another way of telling them that you will not accept this kind of treatment. You are sending the message that what they are doing is not okay and that you want it to stop. Finally, speaking up also shines a spotlight on the behavior so that others can see it for what it is. This will make the gaslighter realize that their techniques are not going to be effective and that their behavior is not worth the condemnation they will receive from others.

Safety First

While there are these benefits to calling out and confronting a gaslighter, it is also a completely valid choice to decide not to speak. Choosing not to engage with an abuser is understandable, and it is entirely up to you whether you want to speak out.

It can be dangerous to show such explicit resistance to an abuser. If you are afraid of what might happen if you speak up, this is a good sign from your intuition that it would not be safe for you to do so. Abusers are desperate to control you and the situation, and if they feel like they are losing their grip, they may escalate their tactics. Physical violence is a real possibility with many gaslighters, and you should always prioritize your safety. If you think that speaking up will get you hurt or lead to severe emotional damage, then it is in your best interest not to.

In that case, this chapter may not be for you. Instead, you can skip ahead to Chapter 5 and learn about how to put distance between yourself and your abuser. Better yet, you can focus on Chapter 6, and start thinking about how to safely leave the relationship. Any situation involving physical violence and emotional abuse is worth getting out of, and you deserve to be safe and happy.

Remain Confident

Keeping the risks in mind, if you do decide to speak up against gaslighting, here is how—remain confident in your reality.

When calling out a gaslighter, don't give in to the urge to question yourself or doubt what you remember. This is what the gaslighter will try to get you to do, so it is crucial to stay firm in your version of reality. Your mind does not fabricate entire events out of thin air, and if you know that you recall something happening in a certain way, then you are likely correct. It is normal to misremember small details, especially from traumatic, abusive, and emotional experiences, but don't let the gaslighter use these little things to trip you up. Stay focused on the bigger picture, and be confident in your own memory, opinion, and judgment.

The goal is to assertively state what you know happened or what you are feeling. You can also present proof of your side of the story if you have any (see Chapter 5 on how to gather evidence). It is important to be tactful here, and try not to turn this confrontation into a "got you" situation. You want to encourage the gaslighter to back down, so don't make them defensive by outright accusing them. Instead, simply give your version of events, and be vigilant about any manipulation tactics that they may use in response.

Prepared Responses

Since you are dealing with a gaslighter, they will likely try to gaslight you when you call them out. Remember from Chapter 2 how these individuals are experts at turning the tables and changing the subject. As such, it is vitally important to be mindful and critical of how they react. There are also some prepared responses that you can have on hand if you notice them engaging with one of their many tools and tactics of manipulation.

For example, if they try to dismiss and trivialize your emotions and concerns, you can respond with something like, "If you continue to minimize what I am saying, then I can't keep participating in this conversation." Or, you can be more direct about your needs and say, "Your feelings are valid but so are mine, and I would really like you to acknowledge my experience." Moreover, if you think the gaslighter is trying to manipulate you further by lying, omitting details, or distorting the truth, you can show them that you are confident in your memory: "I know I'm not imagining what happened," "Being honest with me is the best way for us to understand one another," or "I know what I remember."

The gaslighter may also try to discredit and insult you to change the subject or get you to back down. You can reply to this distraction with something simple and straightforward like, "Insulting me isn't going to make me forget what we're talking about." Similarly, if they try to use backhanded compliments or nasty jokes to undermine you, you can feign ignorance and ask them to explain what they mean. "I don't understand why that's funny" will force the gaslighter to either admit that it was more of an insult than a joke or to back down and retract the comment.

What Not to Do

In addition to staying confident and preparing responses to a gaslighter's defense, you can also be mindful of certain things not to do when speaking up.

Often, the way in which you say something is more important than what you are actually saying. This is why being confident is the cornerstone of confronting a gaslighter. It is also crucial to avoid any type of aggression. You should be careful not to use aggressive language, like sarcasm or insults, and you should make sure that you are not using posturing in your tone and body language. Instead, stick to the facts, and try to project confidence and calm. Don't shout or raise your voice, keep your shoulders back and your head up, and remember to make eye contact.

Getting Emotional

On the note of being calm, you should also be careful not to get visibly upset with calling out a gaslighter. This can make your abuser feel vindicated and validated (remember the warped enjoyment they get out of their manipulation). You also don't want to give them a reason to call you crazy and irrational or to say that you're overreacting.

To maintain your composure, it is best to be careful in choosing when and where you will confront the gaslighter. Make sure that you are fully prepared and feeling emotionally strong and that you have chosen to have the conversation in a place where you feel safest.

Not becoming too emotional doesn't mean that you should ignore your feelings altogether. In fact, when calling out a gaslighter, it is actually better to focus on your emotions rather than the situation itself. This is because it is harder for a gaslighter to dispute what you are feeling than what you remember. They have spent a lot of time and effort getting you to doubt your recall and perception, and they have likely been quite successful.

On the contrary, it is much more difficult for them to deny that you are feeling a certain way. For example, if you know that you are sad and angry, they will have more trouble getting you to believe that you are not than they would have convincing you that you remember something incorrectly.

Exit, Don't Escalate

Perhaps the most important thing not to do when confronting a gaslighter is to escalate the situation. This means being very careful not to get drawn into a conflict. If the other person is not responding to your efforts to engage with them or continues to challenge you, rather learn to let it go than allow the situation to get out of hand.

Unfortunately, this is an outcome that you should expect and prepare for. Because gaslighters are so adept at their manipulation tactics, it is unlikely that speaking up is going to get them to back down. It is vital to keep this in mind, and you should focus on speaking up for your own benefit. You are calling out the behavior to show that you are awake and aware. Your goal should be to prove to yourself that you are grounded in reality and that you know what is happening around you. Instead of expecting an apology or hoping for an argumentative victory, use calling out and confronting as a way of honing your manipulation-spotting skills.

Above all, remember that arguing and tension can put you in a more vulnerable position. Abusers will do anything to maintain control and power, so it is crucial that you do not allow the situation to escalate. One way of de-escalating is simply to pause the discussion. If you feel like you are losing control, say that you need a break and step away from the conversation. You can commit to revisiting the issue later, or you can just physically leave—whatever you need to do to protect yourself.

Ultimately, it is not actually your responsibility to argue with gaslighter, to fix them, or to make them see the error of their ways. They are making a choice about how to behave and treat you, and sometimes, distance is the best option in order to prioritize your emotional well-being and physical safety.

Setting Boundaries

Outside of confrontations and call-outs, the best way to deal with a gaslighter is to set firm and healthy boundaries. You need to communicate to this person what you will accept in a relationship and the kind of treatment that you will not tolerate. The foundation of this is believing that you are deserving of a happy and healthy relationship and acknowledging that gaslighting is unacceptable.

When setting boundaries, it is a good idea to start by being clear about your own needs and expectations. Your feelings are real and valid, and your expectations for a relationship without abuse and manipulation are rational and entirely reasonable. Make sure that the other person is aware of this. Tell them that you will not allow them to minimize and trivialize your emotions or to deny your experiences. Be clear that you are your own person, able to make sound judgments and decisions, and that you will not compromise your entire sense of self for them.

Priorities

Another way to set firm boundaries is to be mindful and respectful of your own time and energy. It is important to make sure that you are not always sacrificing for the gaslighter. Relationships need balance and compromise, and you can't always be the one to give up, give in, and go with the flow.

So, ensure that you are thinking carefully about how you interact with the gaslighter, and try to focus on making healthy choices in this regard. Stop putting them first all of the time when they don't prioritize you in the same way, and stop forgiving them when they won't apologize or keep repeating the same behavior.

These boundaries are particularly important when you find yourself in a relationship with a gaslighter that you cannot avoid, leave, or cut off completely. Common examples of these situations include having to co-parent with a gaslighter or having a gaslighter in your immediate family. In these instances, it is best to focus on limiting and restricting your interactions with the abuser. You should only engage with them when absolutely necessary, and you should keep your interactions centered on the unavoidable reason for the ongoing relationship (for example, the child you are raising together). You can also try to make these interactions as healthy and safe as possible by refusing to be drawn into conflict, walking away when you feel you are being manipulated, and prioritizing your own well-being.

Ultimatums

In addition to setting out your needs and expectations in a relationship, it is vitally important that you establish consequences for someone who does not respect your boundaries.

In the end, your boundaries are quite meaningless if there are no repercussions to crossing them. More than anything, if you set out a clear line about how you want to be treated and then accept someone stepping over it, you will be even more vulnerable to manipulation and abuse. The gaslighter will start to think you don't mean what you say, which will allow them to justify disregarding all of your boundaries and needs. Moreover, they will use your passivity as a weapon, and they will make you out to be weak and indecisive.

So, you need to be firm, and explain to the gaslighter that if they do not respect your boundaries then you will leave. You can give them a simple ultimatum: "Stop disrespecting and abusing me, or I will walk away."

Of course, this is easier said than done. As we have seen, the nature of gaslighting relationships is that victims genuinely trust and love their abusers. It can be incredibly difficult to threaten to leave someone that you care for. But this is precisely why it is so effective. Narcissists will not even consider the possibility that you will walk away, and gaslighters think that they have you tightly under their control. You have the power to prove them wrong and take back your life.

If the abuser is not willing to change and to build a healthy relationship with you, then you must not waver in your ultimatum. You must follow through and leave for your own sake. By giving them a choice, you have given them a chance. You are not responsible for their actions, and if they continue to manipulate and abuse you, then it is time to go.

If leaving seems impossible, keep reading, because the next chapter will provide you with the stepping stones to getting out. It will help you gain distance, space, and perspective, and by the time you reach Chapter 6, you should be ready to learn how to get out of your toxic relationship.

CHAPTER 5:

GAINING DISTANCE AND PERSPECTIVE

As we have explored, a gaslighter's goal is to distort your reality and isolate you from others. They want to make your world smaller so that they can shape it to their liking and benefit. Gaslighters try to undermine your perspective so that you can't understand what's happening, and they cut you off from others so that you can't find your way out of the toxic situation they have created.

This chapter outlines how you can combat these efforts by a gaslighter. It highlights the importance of gaining space and distance to allow yourself to calm down and think clearly. It also emphasizes how you can rely on your existing support network for comfort and an outside perspective. Finally, this chapter will guide you through how to conduct to a reality check for yourself by gathering evidence against the gaslighter.

Stepping Away

To follow on from what we discussed in the previous chapter, often the best option when dealing with a gaslighter is to get some space. The emotional abuse and psychological manipulation of gaslighting naturally evokes very intense emotions. Anger, worry, frustration, confusion, sadness, and fear are all valid responses to an interaction with a gaslighter, but they can negatively affect your mental health and behavior. As such, sometimes, it is better just to walk away.

The gaslighter is unlikely to see things from your perspective, and trying to force the debate will leave you feeling frustrated and angry. Taking a break from the issue at hand can allow you the space and time to calm down. You can work on regulating your emotions and re-establishing a sense of peace. Moreover, once you are back to feeling rational and in control, you will be more capable of addressing the problem effectively. Most importantly, stepping away prevents the situation from escalating to more manipulation and even violence.

The easiest way of escaping a conversation is to commit to returning to it later. For example, if you're looking for an exit strategy from an unending and stressful argument, you can say something like, "Let's talk about this again some other time." You can also be more direct with the person and tell them that you need a break from the interaction. If you want to focus on keeping the peace, you can say, "We don't seem to be seeing things the same way. Let's drop it for now." Then, you can physically walk away.

Putting physical distance between yourself and the gaslighter in these moments is important. To do this, you can simply go into the next room and close the door. Or, you can go out for a walk, take yourself for coffee, or visit a friend. If you feel like you need a lot of time to destress and process your heightened emotions, consider a longer outing like watching a movie at the cinema or staying the night with family.

Give It Some Thought

In addition to providing space and time to calm yourself down, distance from a gaslighter can help you to see things more clearly. Gaslighters are constantly working to warp your sense of reality, and if you can get away for a while, then you can start to regain an objective perspective on the situation.

You can do this by simply thinking more about what is happening to you. Begin with the incident that you are currently taking a break from, and ask yourself what occurred to spark the conflict. Were you trying to speak up and call out the gaslighter's behavior? What was your strategy, and did confronting the gaslighter help or make things worse? How do you feel now? What would you do differently next time? Did you feel like the other person was trying to gaslight you in the moment? Could you spot the tool they were using to manipulate and confuse you? Did it work?

It's important to take the time to think about these aspects of your interactions with the other person more carefully. Take advantage of the time out to get back in touch with reality, and try to see through the abuser's words and actions to get at the heart of the situation. To do this, you need to ask yourself a few key questions about the relationship itself. Are you happy? Is this healthy? Do you feel safe and validated? Why, or why not? Most importantly, do you want things to change?

Suggest a Break

If the answers to these questions lead you to want even more space and distance from the gaslighter, then follow this instinct. You can suggest a break in the relationship to give yourself additional time and space to think things over. The more time you spend away from the gaslighter's deliberate efforts to confuse you, the easier it will be to regain perspective and objectivity. You can begin to see the truth of the abuse, and the different impacts of gaslighting on your perception, beliefs, and behavior will become more apparent.

Again, it is vitally important to be cautious and to put your own safety first. If you feel like telling the abuser that you want to take some time away will instigate a dangerous situation, then hold off. Your fear is a sure sign that leaving the relationship completely is the safer option. In this case, you can jump straight ahead to Chapter 6 for guidance on how to get away from an abuser.

Lean on Others

Another really effective way in which gaslighters try to undermine your perspective is by isolating you from others. These abusers do not want you speaking out about their behavior because they want to maintain power and control over you and your perception. They don't want to give someone else the opportunity to point out their abuse, and they want you to believe that you have no support.

A gaslighter's overall aim is for their victim to stay trapped in the toxic relationship and to never ask for help. But anyone who thinks they are a victim of gaslighting can and should seek out support.

Spot the Problem

One way to combat the efforts of a gaslighter to isolate you is to be more critical and conscious of these actions. Just like with recognizing the other signs of this abuse, you should try to spot how the gaslighter works to cut you off from others.

They might start by simply getting irritable when you go out with friends. Maybe, they become sulky and upset when you choose to spend time with other people instead of them. They may tell you that you aren't taking this relationship seriously, or they might try to convince you that they should be the most important person in your life. The gaslighter's goal with these tactics is to guilt-trip you into prioritizing them while neglecting your other relationships.

Eventually, gaslighters will show their controlling nature more clearly by wanting to know absolutely everything about these other relationships. For example, they will ask you who you are texting with and who you are talking to when you're on the phone, and they will want to know all of the details about who you are going to see. Gaslighters will also engage in more explicit discrediting of your friends and family in an effort to get you to stop spending time with them. They might say that your loved ones aren't supportive and don't want what's best for you. Ultimately, the gaslighter's aim is to be the only one you love and trust.

On that note, it is also crucial to be aware of any way in which you might be aiding these efforts. Specifically, you need to be careful about any forms of self-imposed isolation. Gaslighters are experts at making you feel like you can't talk to others about your relationship. The shame, confusion, and doubt that they create makes it almost impossible to explain what's going on, and it is often easier just to give up on trying. As a result, you start to withdraw from relationships and avoid others. You withhold information and details, make excuses for the abusive behavior, and even defend your abuser.

Over time, you may find yourself siding with the gaslighter over the family and friends that you have trusted all your life. The danger in this is that you can actually be left with no one to talk to aside from the very person who is actively trying to manipulate and control you—which is what the gaslighter wanted all along.

Getting Support

But there is still a lot that you can do to prevent this isolation. Once you have pinpointed the gaslighter's tactics, you can be more cautious about maintaining your support network. You don't have to let your abuser dictate who you see and what you do, and you don't have to let them convince you to isolate yourself and withdraw from your loved ones.

You can counteract these efforts by actively involving people that you trust in your relationship with the gaslighter. Start by talking to them about what you are going through and confiding in them about the truth of your relationship. You can start small and mention just one thing the gaslighter has done and how it has upset you. The goal is to open up and begin a conversation, and you should focus on allowing yourself to be comforted and supported.

It can be helpful to be more direct and deliberate about getting support when you're just starting out. Be sure to choose a family member or friend who you know will respond in a useful and kind way. You can also begin the conversation by saying that you need to talk and asking them just to listen for now. The idea is for you to get used to talking about your relationship and how it makes you feel.

It is only when you get more comfortable that you should start to ask for advice and input. This will ensure that you do not get defensive right off the bat and that the person you have chosen to confide in doesn't try to fix too much too soon.

Backlash

When getting support from your existing network of loved ones, try not to worry about the "consequences" of speaking out. Being worried that the other person will be upset that you're discussing them is a red flag in and of itself. Moreover, as mentioned, gaslighters are excellent at making you feel guilty about talking about them. They are good at playing the victim, and they will most likely accuse you of trying to make them look bad. It is also common for gaslighters to try to change the subject by calling you a liar or a gossip or by telling others that you just want to start drama.

It is important to remember that this is how gaslighters work. Discrediting is a favorite tool, and they will try to destroy your narrative and character by making you the bad guy. It is nothing more than an effort to distract you from their behavior and to avoid responsibility. Above all, it is meant to silence you and to stop you from speaking out.

The first step to coping with this is to expect it. Gaslighters are predictable in their tactics, and they will most likely respond negatively in this way if you try to get support from others. The second step is to pay this backlash no attention. You are not a vindictive gossip, and you are not spreading rumors and telling tales. You are talking to those you love and trust in order to get support. You have every right to do this, and moreover, you deserve this comfort and refuge. Don't let the gaslighter convince you otherwise.

An Outside Perspective

In addition to providing comfort and support, your family and friends can also help to clear up a lot of the confusion and doubt you feel as a result of your gaslighting experience. They can provide an outsider's perspective on the situation, and can do what the gaslighter has been trying to prevent all along—reveal the truth of your abuse.

Your family and friends have the emotional distance to see things about your relationship that you cannot. They can give insight and input that you can't come up with on your own because of how close you are to the situation. Of course, this is not your fault, and is the deliberate intention of the gaslighter. But it is also what makes speaking out so important. Your loved ones will likely be upset on your behalf, but they can still offer an unbiased, third-party view of the situation. They can help you figure out which behaviors are objectively toxic and why, and they can show you that the relationship is manipulative and abusive. Family and friends can also offer rational guidance and advice on how you can proceed.

Moreover, your loved ones can start to undo a lot of the effects of gaslighting by reinforcing that you are not crazy or making things up. They have not been subject to the gaslighter's behavior in the same way as you have, and so, they will have a much firmer grasp on the truth. These support networks are your lifeline to reality, and talking through your experiences and feelings with people who truly want the best for you is another step on your journey of recovery.

Gather Evidence

A final way to combat a gaslighter's attempts to undermine and warp your perspective is to gather evidence on their behavior. They are deliberately trying to get you to lose touch with reality, but you can counteract this effort by having proof of your memories and experiences.

Gathering evidence on a gaslighter involves recording what happens as it happens so that you can come back to this proof when you start to feel the doubt and confusion creep in. You can use your evidence to prove to yourself that you are not misremembering or imagining things. The act of documenting will allow you to track reality, which can shine a spotlight on any lies and misinformation that the gaslighter tries to feed you. Moreover, having objective evidence is useful if you want or need to pursue legal action against the gaslighter one day.

In most cases, however, the primary goal of documentation is to reality check. You are collecting facts and information on your own experiences so that you can reassure yourself about the validity of your memory and perspective. Gathering empirical evidence, recording hard facts, and documenting your own life is the most effective way to build a case for your own sanity. Even if you never need to use this proof against the gaslighter, its very existence can restore your peace of mind and help you understand and process the truth of your experience.

Now that you know the reasoning behind it, you can consider simple ways to gather evidence on the gaslighter:

+ Keep a secret diary in which you record the times, dates, and details of important events, discussions, or experiences. Try to summarize conversations with direct quotes as it can be useful to know exactly what was said. It is also harder to remember emotions as time passes, so try to include descriptions of how you were feeling at the time.

+ Take photos of things that might be relevant, including images of damaged property or physical abuse.

+ Save voicemail messages, memos, and voice notes. Use a recording device or download a recording app to record and save conversations and phone calls.

+ Screenshot, save, and archive text messages and social media interactions that you think may be important later on.

Cover Your Tracks

Once again, safety is vitally important. All abusers want their behavior to remain private, and they are not likely to react well if they find out you are tracking and documenting their abuse.

It is essential that you prioritize your safety when gathering evidence, and it is also a good idea to be generally cautious about how much access the gaslighter has to your life. There are a number of small ways in which you can cover your tracks and protect your privacy:

+ Keep any hard evidence (like your diary) hidden or locked away in a drawer or safe.

+ Regularly erase the search history on all of your devices, especially if you have been researching and reading about abuse and gaslighting.

+ Keep your devices locked away and password protected.

+ Make sure that notifications are turned off so that no one can see messages on your device screen without having to unlock it.

+ Make copies of your digital evidence (photos, messages, voice memos), send these copies to a trusted friend, and then delete your own version so that the evidence cannot be found by the gaslighter.

CHAPTER 6:

LEAVING A GASLIGHTER

The previous chapters of this book have helped you to spot the tools and tactics of gaslighting and to recognize the various signs of this abuse. They have outlined tips for combatting manipulation such as speaking out against your abuser and gaining distance, support, and perspective.

While all of this information and guidance is vitally important on its own, it also provides a crucial foundation for the main message of this chapter. You can—and should—be knowledgeable about gaslighting and able to counteract its methods, but there is really only one definitive strategy for escaping this emotional and psychological abuse.

The most effective way to stop gaslighting is to end your relationship with the gaslighter.

The hard truth about these abusers is that they do not change. Your relationship is unlikely to improve, and the gaslighting abuse will not stop entirely—no matter what you do. As such, this chapter highlights why you should leave, and it outlines how to escape from this situation safely. It also discusses what to expect from the gaslighter in this scenario and how to resist their efforts to make you stay.

Getting Out

In Chapter 1, we explored why some people choose to gaslight others. These individuals often have certain personality traits that predispose them to this kind of abuse, but more commonly, they have learned that this manipulation is an effective means of gaining control. Crucially, they have also not learned any other way of interacting with others. Gaslighting is their primary form of connection, and because it is so ingrained in their psychological and behavioral makeup, they are unlikely to get better.

In other words, gaslighters do not change. This is who they are and have always been, and they will not admit that there is anything wrong with that. They enjoy the power that they hold over others, and in many situations, their gaslighting is effective. So, why would they do things differently?

Ultimately, these emotional abusers lack a certain degree of empathy, and they are not concerned with the impact of their behavior. They value control and dominance over genuine and healthy interpersonal connection, and will gladly sacrifice their relationships in order to maintain power. In truth, their victims are disposable, and if their tactics stop working, they will simply move on to someone else—they will not change their behavior.

The Hard Truth

The implications of all of this can be difficult to come to terms with. Since a gaslighter will not change their behavior, your relationship with them is not going to change either. It will not get better, and the manipulation and abuse will not stop. If you stay in this relationship, you will continue to feel confused, insecure, anxious, and unhappy. You could spend years waiting and hoping for things to get better, but unfortunately, they never will.

Moreover, it is not your job to make them change. Not only is this impossible given their nature, but it is also not your responsibility to "fix" the gaslighter. They are making a choice about how to behave, and it is not up to you to get them to do better. You, and all of their victims, deserve to be treated well, and you shouldn't have to force it out of them. Spending your time running after a gaslighter trying to make them into a healthy and well-adjusted person is damaging and exhausting for you, and it will not work. This is not a case of trying hard enough or "being good enough," and you are not a martyr to be used and discarded by someone who will not take responsibility for their own actions.

Finally, more than anything, it can be dangerous to stay in a gaslighting relationship. Left unaddressed, emotional and psychological abuse only escalates. The manipulation and control intensifies, and the nature of the relationship can turn physically violent—if it hasn't already. As such, even though it can be extremely difficult, getting out really is the best option.

Acceptance

The first step to leaving a gaslighter is accepting that you must. You need to come to the terms with the hard truth discussed above so that your choice to get out is made with confidence and determination.

As with anything, your actions will be more effective if they are self-motivated. It is crucial that you make the decision to leave on your own because you need to be fully grounded in this choice. This is the best way to ensure that you follow through on ending the relationship. It will also provide a more solid foundation for your healing journey. By choosing to leave the gaslighter, you are prioritizing your own well-being and happiness.

To help yourself make this choice, you can start by focusing on what you already know. Have another look at Chapter 3, and work on understanding the different ways in which gaslighting has negatively affected your life. Help yourself to acknowledge that what you have experienced is abuse and that, most importantly, it was not at all your fault. You didn't do anything wrong, and you are worthy and capable of recovering.

Professional Help

In addition to your own personal efforts at processing your experience, you can also reach out for professional help and support.

You can start by visiting your primary care physician who will refer you to a licensed counsellor, psychologist, or therapist. There are mental health professionals who specialize in relationships and abuse, and these experts are best placed to help you begin to accept your situation. A therapist can show you the truth behind the gaslighter's manipulation and abuse. They can provide you with unique tools to cope with the stress and anxiety it causes, and they can give you an outsider's view and professional perspective on the situation.

There are also other professional resources available to you in this regard. You can call a domestic violence or abuse hotline and talk anonymously about your situation. There are local domestic violence organizations that can provide support if you are in need, and online chats or forums can offer a sense of community. Sometimes, it is easier to see the truth of a behavior when it is happening to someone else, and simply having a place to express your feelings and speak about your experience can help you start to heal.

A Safe Escape

The next step to escaping a gaslighter is to physically get out of the relationship. Here, safety planning is incredibly important.

Safety planning refers to tools and strategies that people can use to protect themselves in an abusive situation. This can include having lists of safe places to go, options for escape routes, emergency contact details, and a plan to get away. As with the acceptance step of the leaving process, a professional's guidance is beneficial, and a trained therapist or counsellor will have the experience and resources to help you leave the relationship safely. But if you don't have access to this kind of assistance, there are other options for you—temporary housing at a domestic violence organization, staying with family or friends, or pursuing legal action and protection.

Proper Planning

The most important thing about getting out of the relationship or situation is to have a plan. To start, this means deciding when you will leave and choosing somewhere to go.

If you live with the gaslighter (for example, they are a parent or partner), it is best to choose a time to leave when they aren't there. You don't want to instigate a violent incident, and you don't want to have to fight your way out—emotionally or physically. It is also a good idea to get someone to help you with this process. They can assist you in collecting your necessary things, and can provide emotional support and protection. Moreover, this trusted friend or family member can take you to where you have decided to go.

As mentioned, when leaving a gaslighter, you can find shelter, support, and protection in temporary housing, at a domestic violence organization, or with family and friends. It is crucial that you organize this all beforehand. This may mean doing some research on the local shelters to see if you need to wait for an available bed or if you can just show up. Or, it can mean calling your family and friends and asking them to expect you.

It is always good to have a backup plan in case your first option doesn't work out, so try to have more than one safe place in mind. You don't want to be stuck with your bags in your hand and nowhere to go. You definitely don't want to have to return to the abuser. Whatever the case may be, ensure that your plan is set and ready before you leave.

Tell No One

It is also crucial that you remember to cover your tracks when making your plans. Just as you did when gathering evidence on the gaslighter, you need to protect your privacy for your own safety.

In addition to the tips already mentioned in the previous chapter, you should clear your call log regularly and not save any revealing numbers as named contacts. You can also buy a secondhand and cheap cell phone to use when formulating your escape plan. As long as this device is well hidden, you can program in your emergency and necessary contacts numbers. You should also have the number of the local police or shelter on speed dial if you feel this might be necessary.

Finally, it is best to tell as few people as possible about your exit strategy. You should tell a trusted friend or family member so that they are aware of the situation and can be available in case of emergencies. Otherwise, it is advisable to stay quiet, and you definitely should not mention your leaving to the abuser. As we saw in Chapter 5, telling a gaslighter that you want to break off the relationship can be dangerous, and your safety should always come first. In general, you should be cautious about who knows your plans as you don't want anyone to tip them off. You also don't want to give anyone any opportunity to stop you.

It is safe to assume that the gaslighter will eventually discover that you have left, but the next section will walk you through what to expect when this happens.

What to Expect

Once you have physically gotten out of the relationship or situation, it is crucial that you stay out. The primary goal of a gaslighter is to keep you hooked, and they will do anything to maintain their power and control. You need to be mindful of their narcissistic needs and how effective they are at using manipulation to get what they want.

In short, when you leave a gaslighter, you should expect that they will try to make you stay. There are several strategies that they might employ in order to achieve this. If you can antici-pate these tactics, you will be able to counteract them more effectively.

Playing the Victim

When you end the relationship, the gaslighter will most cer-tainly make themself out to be the victim. They may double down on discrediting you to your family and friends, and they will make you out to be the "bad guy" in this situation. The gaslighter will try to say that it is your fault that the relationship failed and that you are unstable, irrational, or even an awful person. Their goal is to make you feel guilty enough to reach out and reconcile.

Ultimately, there is nothing that you need to do in this situ-ation, except to see this strategy for the manipulation that it is. It is important not to give in to the urge to explain or defend yourself, and don't feel like you need to make sure that every-one understands what really happened. Instead, simply allow yourself to be the villain in the gaslighter's eyes, and take com-fort in the knowledge that the people who truly love you will believe and support you. No one else's opinion matters, and your emotional and mental well-being is more important than the story that the gaslighter choses to tell. Remember that tell-ing tales and rewriting history is what they do best.

Above all, do not be fooled into thinking that you need to discuss any of this with them. You do not need to sit them down and defend yourself. They will not hear what you are saying in any case, and you will just be feeding into their nar-

RECOVERING FROM GASLIGHTING

cissism. They are playing the victim in order to manipulate you, and if you return, you will get sucked back into the same cycle of gaslighting, confusion, and abuse.

Hoovering

Hoovering is another common way in which gaslighters will try to lure you back to them. This is a technique similar to love bombing where they will tell you how much they love you in order to get you to stay.

Hoovering can include excessive praise as well as promises to change. The gaslighter will tell you how much they need you and want you, and they will try to make you feel like you are the most important person in their life. They may even go into detail about how things are going to be different and how they will do better if you give them a second chance. Their goal is to overwhelm you with hope and to manipulate your existing feelings for them. They know that you love them, and they will try to remind you of why. They may reminisce about all the good moments in your relationship, and they will promise to change and make it up to you.

The gaslighter is pulling out all the stops at this point. You need to stay firm in your decision, and you should not to give in to their attempts to suck you back in. It can be difficult to resist promises of love and happiness, but deep down, you know that these are not genuine. The gaslighter won't change because they can't, and if you go back, things will be as they always have. You will not benefit from giving in, and only you can heal the hurt they have caused. Moreover, you deserve to be loved, and this person is not the only one who can do that—despite what they may have told you.

No Contact

Anticipating that the gaslighter will play the victim or try to suck you back in with false promises is a good start, but you can also render these strategies useless by ensuring that they don't have a chance to use them. In other words, the most effective way to stay out of the abusive situation is to avoid exposure to these techniques altogether. This means that you don't give the gaslighter any opportunity to reel you back in.

Ultimately, if you want the abuse to stop, you need to end the relationship, and the best way to end the relationship is to cut off the gaslighter entirely. As such, the golden rule is no contact.

Cold Turkey

Recovering from gaslighting is far more difficult if the abuse is still happening. Complete radio silence can be hard, but having one foot in the relationship means that the gaslighting will continue in some form or another. So, instead of doing things half way, try to let go completely and focus on your healing. You have already made the hard decision to leave for your own health and well-being, and breaking the cycle of abuse is the only way to make that work worthwhile.

Moreover, cold turkey is the most effective option. The gaslighter worked hard to make you dependent on them, and their inconsistent love and attention kept you coming back. But once you cut yourself off from this sparse supply, you can set yourself free. Almost like an addict, you should try to take things one day at a time. Stick to the no contact rule just for today, and then recommit tomorrow.

It is vital to remember that you can't have just a little bit of this person in your life. That is not how narcissists and gaslighters work, and they will want all of you under their control. In order to take your life back, you need to stop engaging completely. You need to let time heal you as you build up days without them. The longer you are away from them, the more control and clarity you will regain.

Block the Number

In a practical sense, no contact involves ensuring that the gaslighter cannot get ahold of you after you have left. This means blocking their number and deleting the contact. You should also block them on social media and email. Don't accept any requests, messages, or calls from unknown accounts or numbers, and make sure that your mutual friends or family are aware that you do not want to hear from the gaslighter.

The only real exception to this golden rule is if your relationship with the gaslighter is unavoidable and they cannot be completely cut off. The primary example here is if you are co-parenting with a gaslighter. The best approach in this case is to limit contact to only what is absolutely necessary. You should set clear boundaries with the gaslighter, and make sure that they understand that your relationship now has a specific and narrow purpose.

Let Go

One useful strategy for maintaining no contact is not to worry about doing "the right thing." You might be concerned that blocking someone is not very kind or that cutting a person out of your life is not a good way to deal with conflict. But the truth is that you do not need to justify the no-contact strategy—not even to yourself.

There is no need to explain to anyone why or how you have chosen to get out of an abusive situation, and you deserve to put yourself first. Remember that you are doing this for your own sake, and it is most likely a last resort. You probably did all you could to make the relationship work, and you do not have to feel guilty for giving up on it.

Similarly, you should try to let go of the need for closure. It might not feel good to end a relationship on such bad terms, but this is your only option. Gaslighters are often incapable of real self-reflection and remorse, and they will never validate your experience like you need them to. It is natural to want an apology or to feel like you should work through what has happened together. But, unfortunately, this isn't possible with an abuser, so you need to change your perspective.

The gaslighter will not give you closure, but you can give it to yourself. You can validate your own feelings about the relationship and how it ended, and you can help yourself work through what has happened. You are capable of moving on and letting go, and the next chapter will show you how.

CHAPTER 7:

MOVING ON AND LETTING GO

● ●

This chapter explores how to start moving on from a gaslighting relationship once you have left. You have done the hard work of physically getting out of the situation, and you have implemented the no-contact rule to ensure that the abuser cannot reel you back in. Now, it is time to focus solely on your own healing and recovery. You can start by learning how to reaffirm your own value.

Gaslighting destroys a person's self-esteem and sense of self, so the best way to begin moving on is to re-establish your own identity and self-worth. You need to accept that you have done nothing wrong, and reconnect with yourself and your life before the abuse.

This chapter discusses how you can do this by highlighting tools like journaling and validating your own emotions. It also touches on how to give yourself closure by letting go of the need to make sense of the relationship. Finally, this chapter looks at forgiveness and grief as important steps for moving on.

Reaffirm Your Value

The foundation of your healing journey should be the understanding that you did nothing wrong and that you are good enough. We touched on this briefly in the previous chapter as part of the acceptance step in the leaving process. Now, let's go into more detail as you move firmly into the recovery stage.

The goal when rebuilding your self-esteem after a gaslighting relationship is to try to see things from a different perspective. The gaslighter worked constantly to make you feel like you were the one that was wrong, irrational, or crazy. They may have even said these things to you outright or blamed you for not being happy in the relationship. At times, it would have seemed like everything was your fault, and that if you could only be better, then things would be okay.

Recovering from gaslighting is about throwing these thoughts and feelings out the window. They do not truly reflect who you are and what you have done. In fact, the opposite is true—it was the gaslighter who behaved badly during your relationship, not you. Gaslighters have a clear pattern of abuse that they repeat across different relationships. They idealize and then devalue their victims in order to confuse and control them. These abusers are a bottomless pit of need, and they can only feel powerful at the expense of others. No amount of control and obedience is enough for a gaslighter. No one is good enough for them.

So, ultimately, it was never about you. You did nothing wrong, and you are not to blame. There was nothing you could have done to prevent the abuse, and there was nothing you did to cause or deserve it. As mentioned, the gaslighter's behavior is their own choice, and you were not responsible for fixing them. You would never have been able to change how they related to you or anyone else, and it was not your job to make them better.

The New Flame

The proof for all of this will be in what the gaslighter does next. After you leave them, you should expect that they will jump right into another relationship. If they cannot get you back, a gaslighter will try to replace you. You need to be prepared for this, and you need to understand that it has nothing to do with you.

Gaslighters are notorious for having affairs, being serial daters, and having several similar relationships on the go at the same time. This is because they like the power, but they are also easily bored and unable to meet their own emotional needs. Gaslighters have endless wants and demands, and no one person can ever fulfill them all. They like to move on from people as soon as the shine of the relationship has worn off. As we've seen, their victims are disposable, and gaslighters shift their attention quickly and frequently so that they can keep themselves in a powerful position.

What this means for you is that you should simply be mindful of these patterns. Don't concern yourself with the gaslighter's new flame, and don't compare yourself to them. Their new relationship has nothing to do with your self-worth, and they will likely repeat the same abusive behavior with the new person. The gaslighter will stay stuck in their own cycle of abuse and manipulation for years, moving from victim to victim, trading love and trust for power and control. They will never get what they think they need. This is not about you, and it is not your problem anymore.

Self-Love

Another way to reaffirm your own value after a gaslighting experience is to make sure that you appreciate your positive qualities. It can be easy to turn to self-blame and shame, but you need to reframe your thinking toward appreciation and self-love in order to heal.

After you leave a gaslighting relationship, you may start to think that perhaps there was something about you that made you more vulnerable to this abuse. You might begin to blame yourself for being too kind or trusting. Maybe, you are actually weak and needy? A pushover? Are you naïve for staying with someone who abused you? A masochist for continuing to care about them? Is it possible that you let this abuse happen?

The answer to all of these questions is a resounding *no*.

Moreover, the only reason you might be asking yourself these things is because the gaslighter spent so much time trying to get you to believe them. They wanted you to question your self-worth and to turn all of your positive characteristics into flaws. The gaslighter needed you to be dependent on them, and destroying your self-esteem was the easiest way to achieve this.

Now that you can see the truth of this, you can take back your perspective. You can get out of this cycle of negative thinking by reaffirming all of the good qualities you possess. Being kind and trusting are strengths to be proud of, and it is not your fault that the gaslighter took advantage of this. They exploited your compassion and empathy, but these characteristics do not make you vulnerable to abuse. You do not need to change yourself going forward or do anything differently in the next relationship. Don't carry this trauma into your future.

Instead, in order to heal from the gaslighting experience, you should work even harder to rediscover all the wonderful things about yourself. Focus on finding your worth again and being who you really are, and remember to stand up for yourself by valuing your characteristics as the positive qualities they truly are.

Reconnect With Yourself

On that note, reconnecting with your identity is another way to affirm your value and move on from this abusive experience. Gaslighting makes you lose sight of yourself and who you used to be. As such, it is important to get to know yourself again—who are you, what do you like, and what do you want out of life?

Journaling

In practice, journaling is a very useful tool for reconnecting with yourself and learning more about who you are. You can purchase a notebook or diary to write in by hand, or you can open up your laptop and type it all out. The goal is simply to start writing about yourself in order to get back in touch with your identity.

You can begin by writing down all of the things that you know about yourself. You can make lists of your likes and dislikes, and you can start by including simple and easy things. Think about your favorite movies, music, and types of food. Give some thought to your hobbies and the things you like to do. Write about anything and everything you know that you don't like.

Next, try to delve deeper into your character, and write about who you are. What are your strengths and weaknesses as a person? What do you value in yourself and other people? What do you believe in? You can also use this as a chance to explore where you are in your life. What are your dreams and aspirations? Do you have any goals that you want to achieve?

As you practice writing regularly, you will find that the words come easier. It may take time, but slowly, you will begin to recognize yourself again. You will feel more sure of who you are and far more grounded in your life and your reality. Your journaling can also give you some direction and purpose for the short term so that you don't feel so lost.

Put It Into Words

Once you feel confident in this recovery tool, you can direct it toward your gaslighting experience. Writing about the relationship and its abuse is an excellent way to process what has happened.

Putting feelings and thoughts into words can make them easier to understand and deal with, and once they are out of your head, you can start to accept and cope with them. Moreover, having somewhere to put all of these emotions can allow you to stop overthinking and overanalyzing. It is important that you remember to take your time when working through the gaslighting experience and to focus on how the abuse made you feel. In doing so, you can help yourself to gain perspective and closure, and this is the cornerstone of letting go.

It is also crucial to stay positive and empathetic in your writings. You should emphasize how much you have grown and what you have learned from the experience instead of trying to pinpoint what you could have done differently. Treat yourself as a survivor, and give yourself the credit you deserve for making it through such a difficult and dark period of your life.

Validating

You can also work to reconnect with yourself and reaffirm your value by validating your own feelings and thoughts. Gaslighters are experts at making you feel like your needs don't matter. They like to trivialize your emotions and undermine your experience so that you will rely on them to shape your reality.

The result is that, over time, you also begin to believe that your thoughts and feelings are irrelevant or even imaginary. You may echo the gaslighter by telling yourself that you are overreacting or being too sensitive. Even after getting out of the situation, you may tend to bottle up your emotions, and you might have trouble expressing what you want, need, and feel.

To undo all of this, you can practice being more conscious of your own experience and accepting yourself the way you are. This means allowing yourself to think and feel freely and not criticizing or questioning what you are doing. So, instead of wondering why you might be feeling a certain emotion or reacting in a specific way, you should simply validate the experience for yourself.

Affirmation

You can do this by verbally confirming what is happening. For example, you can use mantras and affirmations such as, "I know my reality," "This emotion is valid and real," and "I acknowledge and accept my needs in this situation." You can also stay in touch with reality by talking yourself through a situation. If you start to feel the familiar confusion and doubt caused by gaslighting, focus on the facts in front of you. Explain to yourself what is happening, and allow yourself to be comforted by the objective confirmation of your experience.

Validation can be used as a tool in your everyday life, but it is especially important when you are working through your gaslighting experience. As such, you can use this practice in conjunction with your recovery journaling. When you feel compelled to replay situations over and over again or become confused and upset about what has happened, take a break and validate this experience.

You can explore these needs and emotions by writing something like, "My emotions were denied for so long, so it makes sense that I'm struggling to process what I'm feeling right now. I can trust myself, and with practice, I will get better at understanding what I am going through. I don't have to doubt myself or obsess anymore."

Let It Make No Sense

Another crucial part of your healing journey is related to this last point. In addition to trying to process what has happened, recovering from gaslighting also means allowing a lot of the experience to make no sense. Just as you have learned to let go of the need for closure from the gaslighter, you should also let go of the need to understand absolutely everything about your abuse.

Gaslighting relationships make no sense, and this is by design. These situations are founded on manipulation and distorted realities, and gaslighters deliberately try to confuse you and warp your perspective. You will have scattered and fragmented memories of the relationship. Your recollection of events will be out of order, and you may still be doubtful and confused about whether certain things happened the way you think. This is entirely normal. It is a natural response to trauma and abuse, and it is compounded by the gaslighter's intentional efforts to get you to question everything.

Going forward, it is pointless and exhausting to try to remember every detail exactly right and to riddle out precisely what happened and when. You will not be able to, and you also do not need to. There is only so much good that can come from thinking about, working through, and revisiting the experience. Processing your abuse will only get you so far in your healing.

Instead of wrapping yourself up in knots about what really happened and getting frustrated when you can't figure it out, you are allowed to let some things go. You don't have to spend your days obsessing over timelines and trying to reason out the who, what, why, when, and how of it all. The truth is you don't need all of these answers to move on. As long as you focus on accepting that the situation was abusive and you did nothing wrong, you can get closure.

Of course, this is easier said than done. When you find yourself getting stuck in the weeds, just take a deep breath. Notice what you are doing, accept the futility of your actions, and try to move on to something else. You can repeat a validating mantra or distract yourself with a different task—whatever you need to do to reset your thinking. Ultimately, you need to let some of the experience make no sense in order to move on.

Practice Forgiveness

Finally, a really effective way to let go of a relationship is to practice forgiveness. Forgiving what happened does not mean that you are conceding that the abuse and manipulation was acceptable. It does not mean that you are taking any blame.

Rather, practicing forgiveness is about giving yourself permission to forget, heal, and move on.

Forgiveness means giving up hope that the situation could have worked out differently. It is an effort to stop wishing that things would have changed, and it means letting go of the fantasy that everything could have been okay. Forgiveness is about accepting that the relationship was bad from the start, and it goes a long way toward helping you achieve closure. Practicing forgiveness means reinforcing that you are not to blame and accepting that there was nothing you could have done.

The most important thing to remember about forgiveness is that it is for you and not for the gaslighter. You are forgiving what happened for your own well-being so that you can let go of all of the "what-ifs." You are stronger because of what you have learned from the experience, and holding on to the hurt only hinders your growth. Your healing journey does not need grudges or resentment, and letting go of these negative emotions will facilitate your recovery.

Grief

Allowing yourself to grieve is one way to begin this journey of forgiveness. It is important to let yourself feel all of the difficult emotions of loss, anger, guilt, and regret so that you can start to work through them. You cannot process something until you have acknowledged its existence, so you need to be honest with yourself about how much it hurts.

It is okay to mourn the loss of a relationship, even if it was a toxic and abusive one. Just like with forgiveness, being sad to leave a gaslighter does not mean that you accept their behavior, and loving and caring about this person doesn't make your weak. In a way, you are also grieving the person you used to be. You are coming to terms with what you have lost and everything that the gaslighter tried to take from you.

So, give yourself permission to scream and cry over everything that has happened. Create a safe space for yourself, and validate whatever it is that you might be feeling. Allow yourself to be upset and angry, and make sure to tell yourself that any reaction is valid and real. You cannot be numb and shut down forever, and you deserve to express what you are going through in any healthy way that you like.

CHAPTER 8:

TRUSTING YOURSELF AGAIN

The previous chapter focused on the impacts of gaslighting on your sense of self, and it explored the way in which this abuse affects how you value your identity. But there is another side to the consequences of gaslighting for your self-esteem.

Gaslighting can destroy a person's confidence and undermine their trust in themself. It leaves them feeling insecure about their ability to function in the world, and forces them to question their judgement and decision-making. Even after they escape from their abuser, victims of gaslighting often continue to believe that they can't do anything right, and they struggle to feel confident about their independence.

This chapter aims to help you undo these effects by learning to trust yourself again. It highlights the importance of listening to your intuition, and it looks at how making your own decisions is a good way to rebuild your confidence. Finally, this chapter will show you that making mistakes can actually facilitate your recovery from gaslighting.

Overcoming Uncertainty

Gaslighting is psychologically and emotionally devastating because it is a deliberate effort to destroy your confidence. Gaslighters get you to question your own judgment, and try to undermine you ability to think for yourself. They do not want you to challenge or leave them, and will do whatever they can to make you feel like you wouldn't survive without them. It is not uncommon for these abusers to take complete control of your life and to make all of your decisions for you. Moreover, by this point, they have damaged your faith in yourself to such an extent that you find it easier to defer to them anyway.

Trust is such an important part of a person's ability to function in the world, and it is trust that gaslighters violate. As we have seen, this abuse is so effective because victims trust their abusers. The exploitation of this trust has significant ramifications, and people who have experienced gaslighting struggle to restore their faith in others and in themselves.

Ultimately, gaslighting leaves you feeling indecisive and insecure. You do not trust your ability to make decisions for yourself, and you feel incompetent and anxious about a future alone. Given your experience, it can be difficult to see yourself as a competent and trustworthy person. You may question whether you are able to make good choices for yourself and if you are able to do the right thing. You worry about how you will cope, and you feel like you can't rely on yourself. It is also easy to start blaming yourself for being too trusting, and it makes sense that you might be scared of ending up in the same situation again.

Recovering from gaslighting means addressing and overcoming this hesitancy and uncertainty. Healing is about learning that you are a capable and strong person who is able to thrive independently. The opposite of gaslighting is having confidence in yourself and believing in the accuracy of your own perception and judgement. It is about trusting and valuing your decisions and not jumping to the conclusion that you are wrong. This journey requires you to rebuild your confidence and faith in yourself, and the best place to start is with your own intuition.

Listen to Your Intuition

Intuition refers to your gut feeling. It is the instinctual response you have to something based on the way your body and mind process the various informational inputs being received.

Intuition is the sense you get when faced with different signals from your external environment. It is a subconscious or initial reaction that is meant to help you know how you feel about a certain situation. Your intuition has a biological and evolutionary purpose, and it is there to indicate danger and keep you safe. As such, listening to these signals is the best way to protect yourself, which is a crucial foundation for learning to trust yourself again.

As a victim and survivor of emotional abuse, it is not surprising if your intuition initially seems a little quiet. The gaslighter's tactics likely silenced a lot of the warning signs that your body and mind tried to send. The nature of gaslighting is that it attacks the core of the self, and this includes your ability to intuit what is and isn't good for you. The intention of the abuse was to confuse your gut feeling and to make you more vulnerable to manipulation. The consistent efforts to overwhelm and undermine your intuition were all part of an attempt to get you to ignore your instincts in favor of the gaslighter's needs and demands. The end result is a lot of self-doubt, but this can be addressed as you begin to reawaken your intuition.

You can get back in touch with your intuition by focusing on its different aspects. That gut feeling that you get is a combination of physical sensations, automatic thoughts, core beliefs, and immediate emotional reactions. You can cultivate faith in yourself by paying attention to each of these factors.

Body

The first sign that your intuition has something to say will be in your body. Something can feel either physically right or very wrong, and you can use these clues to help yourself make a good decision going forward.

A great example of a physical sensation that you might experience in response to a situation is anxiety. Anxiety is a type of fear, and it is an incredibly useful indicator that something might be off. Your body's systems—heart rate, breathing, temperature—are triggered as an evolutionary reaction to stress, and this is a signal that there is potential danger to be wary of. Your body is biologically programmed to protect you in this way, so you need to pay attention to what it is trying to tell you.

You can do this by being mindful of when you feel physically uncomfortable in a specific place or around a certain person. Notice these signals from your intuition, and listen to them by adjusting your actions and behavior. If something or someone is setting off your internal warning signs, then stay away. You can also try to pick up on the reasons why your body might be reacting the way it is, and work on seeing patterns about yourself and the world around you. As you learn what triggers your gut feeling, you will start to trust that your judgement and decision-making can be relied upon and that you can keep yourself safe.

Mind

In addition to bodily sensations, your intuition is also driven by what is happening in your head. Often, we have thoughts that pop into our minds immediately following a situation, and these knee-jerk mental reactions can be very helpful.

You don't have to act on the first thought that you have, but it is a good idea to investigate it. Why did you have it? What could it be trying to tell you about what you have just experienced? See where the subsequent train of thought takes you, and allow yourself to believe that your thinking patterns are rational. The more regularly you engage your critical thinking, the more you will be able to trust your own problem-solving and reasoning skills. Over time, you will learn that you are capable of logical deduction and that your mental instincts are reliable.

There is also a way to confirm the validity of your thoughts. Often, our automatic thoughts are in line with our core beliefs about the world. These fundamental values will go hand in hand with your intuition, and they can tell you a lot about the best way to act in your own interest. Moreover, figuring out how your first thoughts, core values, and gut feelings align will create a solid foundation for building self-confidence. If you know yourself well, you can trust that you will be able to do what is best for you.

Heart

Finally, immediate emotional reactions are also a crucial part of your intuition. In the previous chapter, you learned the importance of feeling freely and allowing yourself to grieve. This is a great start to reviving the emotional side of your gut instinct.

As you go through your daily life and encounter new people and experiences, you can also try to stay mindful of how things make you feel. Your emotional reactions can guide you toward healthy and productive things and away from harm.

You should carry on engaging in activities that make you feel energized and joyful, and you should stay away from things that evoke more negative emotions—anger, sadness, confusion, and doubt.

Your emotional reactions may seem overwhelming and out of place at first, but this is simply the result of being suppressed for so long. The next chapter touches more on emotional regulation, but for now, you can focus on just becoming more attuned to what you are feeling. Like with your first thought, you don't have to act on your initial feelings. They are there as a guide from your intuition to hint at what might be right for you. Your goal should be to use these responses in conjunction with the rest of your intuition indicators to make the best choice for yourself.

Practice

Listening to your intuition is about honoring your body and mind. It can be difficult and even unpleasant at first, but over time, you will learn to trust your natural instincts again.

In practice, you can further sharpen your listening skills by setting aside some time each day to tune into your intuition. Find a quiet spot, and sit calmly for a while. Think about your day, and try to interpret what your body, mind, and heart are telling you about your experience. Consider all of this evidence together, and use it to made decision or form an opinion about something that has happened to you. You can also use your journaling tool as an aid here. Make a list or a mind map of the different sensations, thoughts, and emotions you've noticed, and draw a conclusion about the message from your intuition.

Another way to open yourself up to your intuition is to learn how to nourish and care for yourself. The next chapter will go into detail about self-care and compassion, but for now, know that giving yourself the capacity to grow is vital for amplifying your instincts. You can also create space for this growth by making small changes to your physical environment. Cleaning up and decluttering the areas in which you live and work will help to free your mind and body from distractions. It will be easier to get to the core of yourself and your intuition if you can give this task your full attention.

Finally, if you would like even more structure at the beginning of your intuition journey, you can consider mindfulness meditation. Mindfulness is a philosophy centered on living in the moment. It is about being present and paying attention to what is happening around you. This practice includes guided meditations that involve observing and describing what you are feeling and thinking, and these exercises can be useful for learning to listen to your intuition.

Make Your Own Decisions

As mentioned, it is normal to feel indecisive after leaving a gaslighting relationship. You would have been so heavily scrutinized and criticized by the abuser that you now have little to no confidence in your decision-making skills. You may hear their words echo in your head every time you try to make a choice, and you may struggle with even the smallest of decisions.

This is a natural consequence of your experience, and it is possible to recover. You don't have to continue to be anxious about whether or not you are making the right choices, and you don't have to blame yourself for being unreliable. The simplest way to heal your confidence and trust in yourself is to start making more choices independently and to be more deliberate and conscious in your decision-making.

Start Small

When embarking on this journey, it is best to start small and to work your way up to bigger decisions over time.

Begin by noticing all of the little ways in which you already make your own choices. You actually decide a lot about your life without even noticing it, but you can make these small decisions more powerful by paying more attention to them. This means actively deciding things like when to get up, what to eat during the day, and what time to go to bed. Rather than going through the motions, try to consciously affirm these choices by telling yourself that you know what you like and want. For example, you love seeing the morning light, so you choose to wake up early. You decide to eat well because you believe in nourishing your body. You want to be productive at work tomorrow, so you are going to bed early.

It is all about intention, and making these choices deliberately will reinforce your independence and sense of capability. Over time, you can prove to yourself that you know what is right for you, and you can move on to bigger decisions about your career, relationships, and life goals. Build up your confidence with little steps, and remember to celebrate your freedom as you go along. Your life is now under your own control, and you have your instincts to guide you.

To help yourself along, it is a good idea to record your decision-making journey in some way. You can journal about the choices you are making, or you can ask your friends and family to help you keep track of all of your progress. The goal of this is to be able to troubleshoot and problem-solve as challenges arise but also to highlight how far you have come. One day, you will look back on this decision-making record, and you won't believe how capable, confident, and independent you have become.

Make Mistakes

A final way to rebuild trust and confidence in yourself is to allow yourself to make mistakes. This can be difficult since you were probably hypervigilant about doing something wrong when you were in the gaslighting relationship. In addition to imposing consequences for making mistakes, the gaslighter likely blamed you for everything—even for things that were not your fault. They made you feel like a failure and like you couldn't do anything right.

Moreover, perhaps there is still a small part of you that believes that it was your mistakes that got you twisted up in that abusive situation in the first place. As such, it makes sense that being wrong is a sore spot and something that you want to avoid. But you can take back a lot of your power and control by allowing yourself to fail in different ways.

Messing up is part of being human. It is a normal, and everyone does it. It is okay to make mistakes because it is impossible to do everything right. It is only your traumatic experience that is forcing you to have such high standards of perfection for yourself. You don't trust that your best is good enough, and you have come to believe that making a mistake means you are a bad person.

This is not at all true. The very nature of a mistake is that it is something done by accident. When you make an error or fail in some way, you are not being malicious or vindictive, and you are not messing up on purpose. It happens to everyone, and it will happen to you—more than once. The best way to deal with this reality is to accept it and to get comfortable with it.

Try and Try Again

Of course, it is okay to be upset when you make a mistake. No one likes messing up or failing, but it is also not a moral indictment on your character. You do not have to let it shake the foundation of your self-belief. One mistake (or two or three or even a dozen) doesn't make you a bad person, and it doesn't mean that you are not capable and strong. There is no need to berate or criticize yourself when you fail, and there is no reason to lose faith in your abilities. Instead, you can work on changing your perspective.

Your goal should be to try to see mistakes as learning opportunities rather than judgments on your worth. Look for the chance to grow from what has gone wrong, and give yourself permission to fail again in the future. The only way to improve is to figure out what doesn't work and then to try something else that might. The beauty of independence is that you can always try again. You have the freedom to make a different choice or even another mistake.

CHAPTER 9:

BEING KIND TO YOURSELF

• •

So far, since leaving the gaslighter, you have learned how to reaffirm your value and reconnect with your identity. You are well on your way to moving on and letting go, and the previous chapter added to this foundation by helping you to rebuild your confidence and self-esteem.

Now, it is time to bring all of these pieces of progress together as you focus on taking care of yourself in the aftermath of your abusive experience. Gaslighting is traumatic, and its long-term consequences can include chronic stress, emotional dysregulation, and other symptoms similar to PTSD. As such, it is vitally important to your healing that you find ways to soothe yourself and enjoy your life again.

This chapter starts by exploring self-care tactics and compassion. It then looks at how you can best regulate your emotions when you are feeling overwhelmed by your experience and recovery. Finally, this chapter emphasizes patience on your journey—healing has no timeline, and even if you stumble along the way, every step forward is a victory worth celebrating.

Self-Care

Gaslighting can have significant consequences for your physical and mental health. Chronic stress, anxiety, depression, and PTSD are all possible outcomes for someone who has suffered this kind of emotional and psychological abuse. The experience can be life-altering, and it's important not to downplay its effects on your body and mind.

Going forward, you can heal and recover by refocusing your attention on yourself. Deliberately showing kindness to yourself is one of the most effective ways to undo the consequences of trauma imposed by someone else, and you can counteract the stress and negativity of gaslighting by focusing on self-care.

Self-care refers to whatever you need to do to take care of yourself. It is about maximizing your physical and emotional well-being. This means intentionally engaging in activities that make you happy and help you to handle difficult emotions and situations. A big part of self-care is about being able to look after and soothe yourself, but an equally important aspect is remembering to have fun and to find joy in your life.

In practice, self-care will look different for everyone, and there is no right or wrong way to go about it. Soothing and leisure activities will be unique for each person, so you don't need to worry about what anyone else might classify as self-care. Ultimately, if it works for you, then it is good self-care.

Moreover, in the context of abuse recovery, the goal is simply to craft a different life for yourself—one that prioritizes your well-being. This means finding hobbies and activities and creating a routine that best serves your health and happiness. Remember to take things slowly at first, and try not to make too much change too quickly. Let yourself adjust and grow, and as you learn more about who you are and what you like, you can add to your self-care tactics and habits.

Psychological First Aid

The first aspect of self-care is about looking after your physical and mental health. This means finding things to do that maximize your energy and soothe your mind and soul.

On the most basic level, this includes making sure that you are eating well, exercising regularly, and keeping up with your personal hygiene. But it is also about having ways to cope when you are feeling down, overwhelmed, or stressed out. To grow and thrive as an independent person, you need to be able to meet your own emotional and physical needs. Moreover, when recovering from gaslighting, you will need unique tools to help you deal with the mental health consequences of this abuse.

You can start by making a list of things that comfort you in times of distress. Think about the last time you faced a challenging situation, and try to recall what you did to help yourself feel better. Does it help to wrap yourself up in a big blanket and read a book in front of the fire? Maybe you like to take a long walk to calm down? Do you find that a distracting activity works best when you feel overwhelmed? Remember that everyone's self-care is unique, so as long as it works for you, it can be a part of your psychological first aid kit.

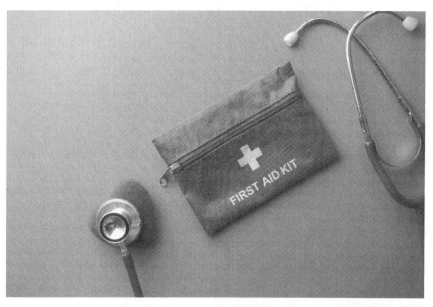

You can also experiment with different self-soothing techniques if you are in need of inspiration:

- ✦ Take a warm bath after a long day.
- ✦ Practice yoga first thing in the morning.
- ✦ Spend time outdoors in nature.

✦ Listen to your favorite music.

✦ Try cooking a new recipe.

✦ Talk to a friend over a cup of coffee.

✦ Light scented candles and sit quietly.

Finding Joy

The second part of caring for yourself is about being able to have fun. It is so important that you try to prioritize leisure and that you make time for the things that you enjoy. Much of your recent experience has been dark, confusing, and upsetting, and it is time to get back into the light.

In practice, this is relatively simple: Just do the things that you enjoy. This means focusing on your existing hobbies and making time to engage in activities that you find fun and relaxing.

For example, if you are a social butterfly, you should make time to hang out with your friends and meet new people. Or, if you enjoy being active, then be sure to get back in the gym or onto a trail. You can go to the cinema to watch that movie you've been waiting for, or you can volunteer your time with a local nonprofit organization. Consider going away by yourself for a weekend or going on a trip to visit your family. If gaming is your thing, then get back online and start playing. If you love spending your time on the beach, at a coffee shop, or in the public library, then go for it. You can also get creative by focusing on art, music, reading, and writing.

Moreover, if are you inspired by any of the things mentioned above, you can try something new and make it an adventure. The most important thing about this type of self-care is that you stay open-minded and enthusiastic. Having fun does require energy and planning, so you will need to put some time and effort into these activities. In the end, however, the benefits will far outweigh any costs. There really is no way to underestimate the value of finding joy again after such a traumatic experience.

Self-Compassion

The cornerstone of self-care is self-compassion. All of your self-care activities and actions—looking after yourself and allowing yourself to have fun—must be driven by a certain attitude. You need to view yourself through a lens of kindness and empathy, and you must handle yourself with delicate love and care.

The goal of self-compassion is to get to a place where you truly believe that you deserve to be treated well. This means engaging with self-care precisely because you see yourself as a person worth caring for. This goes hand in hand with what you learned in Chapter 7 about reaffirming your value, and it is an important step to take when recovering from gaslighting. The abuse was not your fault, and you did not deserve to be made to feel worthless. You can take back your power by eradicating any lingering doubts—you deserve to be loved, valued, and respected, and the best place to start is with how you treat yourself.

Manifesting Kindness

In practice, a really effective way to manifest kindness toward yourself is to be mindful of how you talk to yourself. This means being careful of negative self-talk and working to replace criticism and doubt with compassion and empathy.

Start by noticing how you talk to yourself on a daily basis. There was likely a lot of negativity and criticism in your gaslighting relationship, and the repetition and reinforcement of the abuse can mean that you are still perpetuating this perspective in your own head.

For example, when you make a mistake, is your first thought always something negative? *Oh, I'm such an idiot. I can never do anything right.* Do you talk down to yourself? *I look terrible today. That was a stupid thing to say. I'm awful at this job.* Are you constantly discouraging your own efforts? *There's no use in trying. I'll never be happy. I'm sure I'll mess it up anyway.*

You might not be doing this intentionally, but it is so crucial to pick up on these automatic negative thoughts. They shape your beliefs about yourself, and can have drastic consequences for your self-esteem and confidence. You don't need to be thinking or feeling this way, and part of manifesting self-compassion is about changing how you view yourself.

Positive Replacement

Once you've identified your negative self-talk, you can counteract it more effectively. One way to do this is to fact-check the validity of these thoughts to see that they are not true. This means looking more critically at what has just popped into your head and deciding whether it is an objective fact or just an opinion that needs revising. Facts will be supported by evidence that you can point to as confirmation, but opinions will not be based on any kind of proof that you can see.

Most of your negativity is likely subjective and based on distorted thinking inspired by your abuser, and there is no need to stick to this perspective. You no longer have to believe that you are incompetent, forgetful, irrational, or worthless—you can form a new opinion of yourself.

A great way to do this is to implement positive thought replacement. This is a tool to counteract automatic negative thoughts, and it is very simple and easy to use. As soon as you notice a negative thought or idea, replace it immediately with something more positive. For example, if you make a mistake at work and start to think that you are stupid or bad at your job, try to counteract these thoughts by finding a way to compliment yourself. Think about the last time you did a task really well, and focus on your successes and positive characteristics instead.

Similarly, you can use compassion statements and daily affirmations to create more positivity in your life and mindset. Challenge yourself to write out kind and empathetic messages about your character and abilities, and make goals for yourself that are uplifting and inspiring. You can also use these statements as a way of talking to your inner child or to the person you were when you were stuck in the gaslighting relationship. Imagine that you are having a conversation with this person, and show them compassion and support. This will help you practice comforting yourself, and will allow you to break free of your own mental negativity.

Regulating Your Emotions

Another important aspect to taking care of yourself is being able to process and manage your own emotions. You need to be able to look after yourself emotionally, and you have to learn to meet your emotional needs. This means self-soothing with your self-care activities, but it is also about understanding and controlling your feelings in times of distress.

Emotional regulation is a tool for learning to cope with your own emotional experience. It involves examining what you are feeling and why, and it is a vital technique for being able to tolerate the ups and downs of life. Moreover, emotional regulation is a necessary part of healing from emotional abuse. The gaslighter deliberately manipulated your emotional state and emotional intelligence for their own purposes. They trivialized and minimized your needs, but they also tried to confuse and overwhelm your senses. You would have constantly felt upset and out of control to the extent that you believed yourself to be irrational, immature, and overly intense. Emotional regulation is about taking back your control and building up tolerance for distress.

Identifying and Labeling

Learning how to regulate your emotions will help you to feel safe, calm, and consistent. It allows you more control over your feelings, and it will ensure that you are less overwhelmed by your experiences. Emotional regulation is also important as a way of making you less vulnerable to emotional manipulation in the future. If you feel strong and grounded in your emotional state, you are less susceptible to the needs, whims, and demands of an abuser.

The first step to regulating your emotions is learning how to identify and label what you are feeling. This might sound simple, but you will need to get to know your emotions after they have been suppressed for so long. You might still be confused and uncertain about what exactly you are feeling, which is why knowing your exact emotion can be helpful. Only once you know what it is can you start to cope with it.

In practice, there are several ways to start identifying and labelling your emotions:

- ✦ You can use an emotions chart with mood faces that indicate potential feelings.
- ✦ You can try out a more intricate emotion wheel that describes the different variations and nuances of your emotional state.
- ✦ You can journal about your emotions by focusing on how different experiences and situations make you feel.
- ✦ You can talk to a trusted friend or family member about your emotions.

Whichever method you choose, the most important thing is to be as specific as possible. Practice using descriptive words and finding an exact label that fits how you are feeling. The goal is to be able to name your emotions so that you can properly express what is happening in your head. Instead of bottling up and suppressing your feelings and needs, you want to be able to get them out in the open so that you can confront them.

Building Resilience

After you have managed to put your feelings into words, you can start to process these emotions. Emotional regulation is all about getting comfortable with your feelings—even the uncomfortable ones. It is about undoing the emotional abuse of gaslighting and learning that you can trust your emotional experience.

It is not realistic to aim for constant happiness. You are going to be upset, sad, worried, and angry at some point or another. The goal is not to hide from these experiences but rather to embrace them. As you get used to feeling and coping, you will notice how much easier it becomes, and this emotional resilience is the foundation of mental well-being. You need to rediscover your emotional limits and build up tolerance to distress. This will allow you to bounce back from disappointment, pick yourself up after falling, and continue to grow and learn.

From a practical perspective, building emotional strength is about being mindful. You need to pay attention to your emotions, sit with the discomfort, and not try to run from what you are feeling. You can do this by examining the emotions you have identified and labeled in more depth. Notice how they affect your physical and mental state, and try to figure why you are feeling this way. What has triggered this response? Can you spot a pattern of stressors in your life?

Next, you can work on how you react to your feelings. Think about how you can cope more effectively with life's challenges. Consider your self-care activities, and decide on something that will make you feel better. The goal is to work through this emotional experience—not to walk away from it.

Patience

As with all aspects of recovery, learning to understand and control your emotions will take time. It also requires practice and effort to implement self-care activities, and it may take a while before you start to notice the impact of your self-compassion. Ultimately, healing has no definitive timeline, and you will need to be patient with yourself as you continue on this journey of kindness and recovery.

Think about it this way: The gaslighter worked consistently to deconstruct your entire sense of self. They made repeated efforts to undermine your self-esteem, and the impact of their deliberate abuse cannot be understated. It makes sense that it will take time to rebuild and repair who you are.

Moreover, there is no rush. Healing happens at its own pace, and it rarely happens in a straight line. There will be ups and downs, but as long as you are working on your recovery in your own way, you are making progress. The only requirement is that you keep going. Stick with your self-care, your journaling, and your efforts to understand yourself and your experience. Don't give up hope—recovering from gaslighting is fully possible, and you are strong, capable, and worthy of happiness and well-being.

Re-Encountering Gaslighting

You should also remember to be patient with yourself when you face challenges similar to those you are trying to recover from. You may stumble into a pattern from the past, but a few steps backwards doesn't mean that you aren't healing and doing your best.

It is important to keep this in mind because it is not unlikely that you will encounter gaslighting again. Unfortunately, this kind of abuse and manipulation is common in our modern society, so you need to be vigilant about its tricky manifestations. Gaslighting often rears its ugly head in other areas of our lives, and it can appear in the way in which we talk to one another:

✦ "Don't take it so seriously."

✦ "Everything happens for a reason."

✦ "You need to look on the bright side."

✦ "You shouldn't let things get to you so much."

These are all examples of how society expects us to ignore our own emotions and reactions. We are encouraged to look away from the difficult truths and pretend that everything is fine. In reality, emotions are natural, and it is gaslighting to deny or dismiss these experiences. You can rebel against these little forms of abuse by refusing to minimize the intensity of your own emotions. Recognize this behavior for what it is, call it out, and reclaim your reality.

In the end, recovering from gaslighting is an ongoing learning process. You need to be prepared to re-encounter this manipulation, but you can also rest assured that you have the tools and strength to combat this abuse. Moreover, the final chapter of this book will focus specifically on how to avoid gaslighting in your future interactions. It is all about counteracting similar emotional and psychological abuse at the interpersonal level and building healthy relationships.

CHAPTER 10:

BUILDING HEALTHY RELATIONSHIPS

The final chapter of this book is about undoing the loneliness caused by gaslighting and establishing healthier relationships in the future.

It explores how to recover from the isolation of abuse by returning to your existing support network and creating new connections. It then discusses how you can improve your own interpersonal skills by practicing assertiveness and focusing on communication. Finally, this chapter looks at relationship red flags and warning signs to help you avoid gaslighting going forward.

Undoing Isolation

As we have discussed, one of the primary ways in which gaslighters work to maintain their control over you is by isolating you from others. They discredit you to your loved ones, and manipulate you into withdrawing from the people who care about you. The gaslighter makes you feel like you are alone in the world, and encourages you to choose them over everyone else.

As such, once you move on from this abusive relationship, it may be that you find you have fewer friendships and connections than you did before. Moreover, your trust in the world has been violated by the gaslighter, and it is entirely under-standable that you would be suspicious of others. You may be very hesitant to open up again and prefer being closed off. You have been hurt and exploited, and you don't want that hap-pening again. The idea of being in another relationship makes you afraid, and even just connecting with people as friends, colleagues, and acquaintances seems difficult.

This is okay, and it makes sense given what you have ex-perienced. But it can also be addressed. You can learn to love and trust again, and you will be able to restore the connections you have lost. It is possible to get out of the isolating world of mistrust and fear, and you will find people who feel safe. Throughout this book, you have been working hard on your self-esteem, confidence, and trust, and it is time to put this into practice as you re-enter the world. Moreover, not only are you capable of building healthy relationships, but you should.

The Pros of People

Humans are social beings, and we all need some form of social interaction. Even if you are shy or introverted, you need other people to love and lean on. Socializing is critical to your inter-personal well-being, and you have to engage with others in order to maximize your happiness and health. You can't isolate yourself forever or try to survive on your own, and re-estab-lishing and building healthy relationships will only aid in your recovery from gaslighting.

There are several benefits to socializing and maintaining healthy relationships. It gives you someone to share your ex-periences with and someone to spend time with. It is a great way to incorporate fun and joy into your life, and it is always good to have someone to laugh and joke with. Friends, family, colleagues, and partners are also able to provide emotional support and comfort when you need it. Having someone to talk to can lighten the burden of your troubles and help you improve your own mindset. Forming these connections coun-teracts the depression and anxiety caused by loneliness, and socializing has direct benefits to your physical health. It combats stress, increases longevity, and reduces your chances of chronic illnesses like heart disease and dementia.

The more time you spend with others, the more you will reap rewards for your effort. As you get comfortable opening up, you should notice your capacity for trust re-emerging. Over time, it will be easier to get close to people and to heal from your previous experience. You will also be able support others when they need it, and you will reach a point of being able to return love and comfort more readily. Ultimately, it is possible to overcome the trust and intimacy issues instilled in you by your abusive experience, and you can start this journey simply and slowly.

Start Slow

The first step to re-integrating in society is to start with your existing network of friends, family, colleagues, and acquaintances. In other words, begin with the people you already know, love, and trust, and practice flexing your social muscles in these safe spaces.

It may be necessary to repair some of these relationships, but don't be deterred by this prospect. Remember the main message of this book—you are a victim of abuse, and it is not your fault. If a relationship was damaged during the gaslighting abuse and it is important that you restore it, then just be honest. Open up to this person about what you were going through and how you felt like you had to push them away. Help them to understand why you acted the way you did, and give them your perspective on any conflict that occurred. It is possible to take accountability for withdrawing in this context. It does not mean that you are assuming responsibility for your own abuse. You are simply trying to heal any hurt that was caused as a by-product of the situation.

In addition to being open about your experience, you can also restore your relationships by being intentional at the beginning of this process. You are trying to rekindle your closeness with someone, so it is important that you reach out. Make plans with this person, and put your best effort into rebuilding this relationship.

Finally, you need to spend time healing around people who will lift you up, so be mindful of who you let into your circle in these early stages. Focus on the friends and family members who believe in you and validate your experience, and let go of anyone who does not support your recovery. Move on from the people in your life who side with your abuser or the mutual friends that cannot see your point of view. It can be difficult to have to pick and choose in this way, but you cannot fully heal from toxicity if it is still seeping into your life.

New Connections

It is also always an option to form new connections and to meet new people. You might not feel overly confident about this at first because the gaslighter worked to tarnish your self-esteem. They tried to make your world smaller, but you can take back your life by being open to new experiences again. Remember all the progress you have already made, and focus on what you have learned and how you have grown—you are strong, fun, and worthy of companionship and support.

Moreover, you can go slowly on this journey as well. You don't have to make lifetime connections every day or find yourself a new best friend right away. You can simply focus on having fun, and there are a lot of easy ways to socialize and meet new people:

- ✦ Strike up a conversation with someone at the local park.
- ✦ Hang out at a popular bar or café.
- ✦ Search online forums, websites, and social media pages for things to do in your area.
- ✦ Attend an event like a music festival or open-air movie screening.
- ✦ Volunteer at an old age home or orphanage.
- ✦ Offer dogsitting or babysitting services to people in your area.
- ✦ Join your community group and attend its meetings.
- ✦ Visit a museum or art gallery nearby.
- ✦ Take a yoga or painting class.
- ✦ Enroll in a course at a community college.
- ✦ Join the neighborhood walking, running, or cycling club.
- ✦ Support a local sports team.

Interpersonal Skills

When socializing and maintaining relationships, it is also crucial that you stay mindful of your own interpersonal skills and how you interact with others. You need to be able to communicate well and assert your own boundaries in order to ensure that your relationships are healthy and beneficial.

After experiencing the emotional abuse of gaslighting, you have learned a lot about what is and isn't healthy in a relationship, and you will have a good idea about what you want and what you will not accept. You should have an excellent understanding of what toxicity, gaslighting, and abuse look like, and it is vital to stay firm in this knowledge. You also need to work on putting it into practice in your relationships going forward.

Assertiveness

Assertiveness is an effective interpersonal tool for creating a safe and healthy relationship. It means having the ability to express yourself in a way that is respectful to both parties in the relationship.

The first step to assertiveness is being confident about your own needs and wants. Decide what you are looking for in a friend or partner, and consider what you would need from the relationship in terms of support and trust.

You can also round out your own interpersonal well-being by considering what you have to offer someone else. Figure out your own your strengths and goals, and try to balance what you need with what you can provide. Remember that respect goes both ways, and relationships are built on mutual contribution, compromise, and collaboration. You should be prepared to listen to the other person's experiences and expectations, and you should want to work together to create a healthy and validating space.

Boundaries

Next, you need to be clear about any boundaries that you have when it comes to relationships. Assertiveness is about respectfully making clear what you will not accept from someone else, and this will include aspects of the abusive situation you have experienced.

You don't have to jump right into these intimate details as soon as you meet someone. In general, you can tailor your expectations and boundaries as to the relationship progresses, and once things have settled, you can instigate a more extensive discussion. Of course, if you notice a red flag right off the bat (see the next section), you can try to halt this behavior in its tracks.

On that note, the final aspect to assertiveness is reinforcing and maintaining your boundaries. This means saying no when someone tests your limits and calling out behavior that crosses your lines. It can be helpful to explain to the other person what you have been through and why your boundaries have to be so secure. If you are both on the same page, it is easier for everyone to feel respected.

But, above all else, if someone continues to push and push, then you should leave. You are not obligated to give them another chance, and you are allowed to put yourself first. As long as you were clear about your boundaries, there is no reason to explain yourself or stay.

Communication

Your interpersonal skills are also largely defined by how you communicate, so it is essential that you are mindful of your strengths and weaknesses in this area. Take some time to understand your preferred methods and means of communicating, and make sure that the other person in the relationship is aware of how you like to operate. You should also be willing to acknowledge where you can improve in these skills, and if there is a communication problem, you need to be open to addressing it.

Just like when you were dealing with the gaslighter, speaking up is important in any relationship. You may be hesitant or reluctant given your recent abusive experience, but you can't withhold all of your words and assume someone else will read your mind. You have already learned skills for speaking up in Chapter 4, so you know that you are capable of communicating your needs. If something is wrong, you have to get it out of your head before you can fix it.

When you want to raise such an issue, it is helpful to think carefully about what you want to say before diving right in. You can plan your words in advance if the topic is tricky, and write down a few of your key points. It is also important to make sure that you have a clear outcome in mind for the interaction— what do you want to achieve, and what solutions can you offer? Remember that how you say something is as influential as what you say, so be mindful of your tone and body language. You don't have to be aggressive or accusatory to resolve an argument. In fact, the conversation will progress more smoothly if you are calm, confident, and clear.

If you are particularly nervous about a specific conversation, you can role-play it with another person that you trust. This just means having a practice run at what you want to say and trying out different ways of getting your point across. You can also work on how you will listen and react to what your partner might say.

Keep in mind that the other person might have an entirely different perspective to you, so in order to resolve the problem, you should encourage them to speak their minds as well. Focus on actively hearing what they are saying, and try to react in the same way you would want to be received. If you both work together to create a safe and healthy space, then neither of you should feel any hesitancy or reluctance about having to speak up.

Red Flags

The most effective way to avoid toxicity when building new relationships is to be vigilant about any warning signs that the other person might exhibit. You have a wealth of knowledge about gaslighting, manipulation, and abuse. You lived through that experience, you know how it felt, and you have had it all reinforced by the information in this book. If anyone can spot a red flag, it's you.

It is normal to have occasional disagreements and differences in a relationship, and this is generally not something to worry about. But, as you know, your alarm bells should ring if you start noticing patterns. Gaslighting is about consistency and repetition. It is an ongoing effort to destabilize and confuse you, and it involves regular manipulation on several fronts. This is not a one-off experience, so be wary if you spot the same warning signs popping up over time.

You should recognize many of the most common relationship red flags from your gaslighting relationship:

- ✦ Abusers are often people who won't easily forgive and will continue to hold grudges.

- ✦ They refuse to take accountability or responsibility for their actions, and constantly deny wrongdoing.

- ✦ It is common for them to shift blame on to others, and they often make you feel like everything is your fault.

- ✦ They always put themselves first.

- ✦ When they do something for you, an emotional manipulator will then turn around and blame you for being needy.

- ✦ Potential gaslighters condescend and criticize constantly.

- ✦ They are controlling, and always have to have things their way.

- ✦ Abusers make you feel powerless, insecure, and bad about yourself.

- ✦ They engage in verbal or physical abuse.

Retracing Your Steps

In addition to these red flags, you can also look to yourself for signs of potential toxicity in the relationship. Like you did in Chapter 3, see if you can notice negative changes in your beliefs, self-esteem, and behavior. Do you feel confused and anxious around this person? Do they make you feel like you aren't properly grounded in your past and present? Are you starting to feel unseen, unheard, and dismissed? Have you been avoiding your loved ones so you don't have to talk about it?

If you are ticking a lot of boxes in this section and can feel the déjà vu setting, take a step back. Revisit the earlier chapters of this book, remind yourself of the path out of abuse and toxicity, and retrace these steps. You can call out the negative behaviors, and set stronger boundaries in the new relationship (Chapter 4). Or, you can gain distance and perspective by taking a break and leaning on your loved ones for support (Chapter 5). It is also possible to get out of this potentially dangerous relationship, so go back to Chapter 6 if you want to leave.

Taking Responsibility

The overall idea is to reassess this relationship more carefully in order to determine if you are losing your sense of self. Listen to your intuition in this crucial moment (Chapter 8). You have sharpened it specifically for times like these, so let it do what it was designed for. Allow yourself to be protected by your gut feeling, and follow your instincts. You have been through this before, and now, you know better. Compare how you feel and act in this new relationship to what was happening with the gaslighter, and if you see any similarities, take action.

The most important thing is to be proactive and to take responsibility for your own mental health, emotional well-being, and physical safety. You are informed and experienced enough to make your own choices, and you need to trust that you will do what is best for you. If you think you need to leave and that this new relationship is not worth it, then get out. You have grown and learned so much, and you don't need to rely on anyone else to keep you safe. You know your own worth, and you no longer have to accept any less than you deserve.

CONCLUSION

Having reached the end of this book, you should have all of the tools that you need to escape from gaslighting. Your journey out of emotional and psychological abuse is ongoing, but you have a variety of strategies that you can implement as you continue to heal and recover. This book has given you a wealth of knowledge and practical guidance, and all that is left is for you to take each step as it comes. Remember what you learned, and put it into practice.

You now know that gaslighting is abuse. You understand that it is emotional and psychological manipulation designed to make you dependent and keep you trapped in toxicity. It is a learned behavior that is all about control and predicated on unequal power dynamics (Chapter 1).

You can spot the tools and tactics of gaslighting, and you know that it is founded on lying and deliberate misinformation. Gaslighters rewrite the past, withhold validation, and deny your experiences. They make you question everything, and they expertly change the subject with diverting, trivializing, and stereotyping. You know how they like to turn the tables to make everything your fault, and you can recognize countering, discrediting, and love bombing as the two-faced manipulation that it is (Chapter 2).

Moreover, you are now familiar with the dangerous dynamics of this kind of abuse, and you are aware of how it attacks the core of the self, exploits trust, and reinforces with repetition. You know how gaslighting causes confusion and concern and how it makes a victim blame themself. This abuse makes you feel like you are never good enough, and it has you thinking that you might actually be going crazy. You find yourself apologizing constantly, staying silent and bottling up all your emotions, and giving up your control and independence (Chapter 3).

From a practical perspective, you now know why speaking up about gaslighting is so important. You know how to confront and call out a gaslighter's behavior, and you are aware that you should value your safety above all else (Chapter 4).

You have learned that gaining distance and space is the first step to seeing the truth of the abuse. You need an outside and objective perspective to cut through all the lies and manipulation, and for this, you can turn to your existing support network or you can gather your own evidence against the gaslighter (Chapter 5).

Your journey out of gaslighting would have taken a sharp turn once you accepted that the only real way to stop this abuse is to get out of the relationship. Safety planning is essential when leaving an abuser, and implementing the golden rule of no contact ensures that you aren't exposed to the gaslighter's victimization and hoovering (Chapter 6).

As you continue making progress in your recovery, keep in mind the strategies you have learned for moving on and letting go. It is vital that you reaffirm your value, identity, and positive qualities after an abusive experience, and tools like journaling and validating your own emotions are effective ways to do this (Chapter 7).

You've also seen how important it is to learn to trust yourself again, and building up confidence and a sense of capability is best done by making your own decisions and allowing yourself to make mistakes (Chapter 8). Remember to relish your freedom and independence when you practice these strategies, and keep moving forward on this journey of self-discovery and self-belief.

You know how crucial it is to be able to care for and love yourself in the aftermath of abuse. Self-care and self-compassion are cornerstones to healing, and they can help you find much-needed joy in your life again. Emotional regulation is another useful tool for recovering from emotional abuse, and building up resilience and tolerance to distress is vital for your overall well-being (Chapter 9).

Finally, you have learned that you can't be afraid of relationships forever and that you shouldn't carry your trauma with you. You can rebuild lost relationships and undo the isolation of gaslighting by forging new connections. It is also possible to protect yourself from abuse in the future by being mindful of relationship red flags.

Ultimately, recovering from gaslighting is a continual process. Making it through the chapters of this book is an excellent foundation, and you need to continue working with the information and tools you have explored. Above all, keep in mind the most important message of this book: Gaslighting is abuse, you are a survivor, and you are capable of moving on and healing from this experience.

GLOSSARY

Antisocial Personality Disorder: A mental illness that causes someone to disregard societal rules and expectations and to have little regard for the difference between right and wrong.

Assertiveness: Clearly stating your needs and boundaries in a way that is respectful to both parties of a relationship.

Borderline Personality Disorder: Personality disorder characterized by instability in self-image, relationships, emotional responses, and behavior.

Cold Turkey: To stop doing something suddenly and abruptly.

Countering: When gaslighters evade responsibility by questioning a victim's memory and perception.

Discrediting: Speaking badly about someone to their loved ones as a way of isolating them from others and making them seem untrustworthy or irrational.

Diverting: Tactic used by gaslighters to change the subject of conversation by downplaying the situation and questioning the victim's credibility.

Emotional Regulation: Technique to understand and control your emotions as a way of building up emotional resilience and tolerating distress.

Gaslighting: Type of emotional and psychological abuse that uses manipulation and lies to get someone to question and doubt everything about themselves and their reality.

Honeymoon Phase: Period at the start of a relationship where few problems arise and both parties are happy and carefree.

Hoovering: Strategy used by gaslighters to try and suck their victims back into a cycle of abuse and manipulation.

Intuition: Gut feeling or instinctual response to a situation based on how your mind and body processes the information it receives.

Love Bombing: Using praise, promises, and words of kindness and compassion as weapons of manipulation to maintain control.

Medical Gaslighting: When a medical professional dismisses or downplays a patient's health concerns and symptoms as unimportant or imaginary.

Mindfulness: Philosophy of living in the moment and paying attention to what you are experiencing.

Narcissism: Personality trait that causes someone to have an unreasonably high opinion of themselves and to lack concern for the feelings and interests of others.

Political Gaslighting: When politicians and governments manipulate information and deceive the public about their promises and outcomes.

Positive Thought Replacement: Tool to address automatic thoughts by countering criticism or negative self-talk with something more positive.

Psychopathy: Psychological condition characterized by lack of empathy and other antisocial behavior.

Racial Gaslighting: When gaslighting tools are applied to an entire racial or ethnic group as a way of discrediting and disempowering this sector of society.

Red Flag: Warning sign indicating that a person or relationship may be abusive or toxic.

Safety Planning: Strategies and tools that victims of abuse use to leave an abusive situation safely.

Self-Care: Activities and behaviors that a person uses to cope with distress and to maximize their physical and mental health.

Self-Compassion: An attitude of kindness and compassion that underpins how you view and treat yourself.

Stereotyping: Exploiting existing societal stereotypes and biases to maintain power and control over someone.

Support Network: Group of people in your life that love and support you.

Trivializing: Technique of minimizing and dismissing someone's feelings and needs.

Validate: To show support for something or to confirm its existence, accuracy, and value.

Withholding: When a gaslighter refuses to acknowledge a conversation or situation and will not engage with someone in a meaningful way.

REFERENCES

Drake, K. (2021, June 4). *7 tips to identify and deal with gaslighting.* PsychCentral. https://psychcentral.com/blog/how-to-identify-and-deal-with-gaslighting

Eggshell Therapy and Coaching. (2022, March 3). *Gaslighting and the highly sensitive person (HSP).* https://eggshelltherapy.com/gaslighting-recovery/

Field, B. (2023, April 26). *The dangers of love bombing.* Verywell Mind. https://www.verywellmind.com/what-is-love-bombing-5223611

Goodman, W. (2021, September 30). *How to heal from gaslighting: A therapist explains steps to start your healing process.* The Collaborative Counseling Center. https://www.collabcounseling.com/blog/how-to-heal-from-gaslighting-a-therapist-explains-steps-to-start-your-healing-process

GoodTherapy. (2018, June 13). *Gaslighting. https://www.goodtherapy.org/blog/psychpedia/gaslighting*

Gordon, S. (2023, May 1). *Is someone gaslighting you? Learn the warning signs.* Verywell Mind. https://www.verywellmind.com/is-someone-gaslighting-you-4147470

Greenberg, M. (2021, June 30). *5 go-to tactics of gaslighters, and how to resist them.* Psychology Today. https://www.psychologytoday.com/za/blog/the-mindful-self-express/202106/5-go-tactics-gaslighters-and-how-resist-them

Huizen, J. (2022, July 14). *What is gaslighting?* MedicalNewsToday. https://www.medicalnewstoday.com/articles/gaslighting

Johnson, M. Z. (2016, March 28). *6 unexpected ways I've healed from gaslighting abuse and learned to trust myself again.* Everyday Feminism. https://everydayfeminism.com/2016/03/healed-from-gaslighting-abuse/

Lonczak, H. S. (2020, August 21). *What is gaslighting? 20 techniques to stop emotional abuse.* PositivePsychology.com. https://positivepsychology.com/gaslighting-emotional-abuse/

National Domestic Violence Hotline. (2020, September 20). *What is gaslighting?* https://www.thehotline.org/resources/what-is-gaslighting/

Psychology Today. (2017, November 7). *Gaslighting.* https://www.psychologytoday.com/za/basics/gaslighting

Raypole, C. (2022, June 21). *Think you're being gaslit? Here's how to respond.* Healthline. https://www.healthline.com/health/how-to-deal-with-gaslighting

Sander, V. (2021, December 10). *The health benefits of socializing.* SocialSelf. https://socialself.com/blog/socializing-health-benefits/

Sarkis, S. (2021, March 12). *How to regain your sanity after you've been gaslighted.* MindBodyGreen. https://www.mindbodygreen.com/articles/what-to-do-when-youve-been-gaslighted

Stiefvater, S. (2022, March 10). *7 long-term effects of gaslighting (and how to recover).* PureWow. https://www.purewow.com/wellness/long-term-effects-of-gaslighting

Image References

AbsolutVision. (2017, November 27). *Four green emoticon balls* [Image]. Pixabay. https://pixabay.com/photos/smiley-emoticon-anger-angry-2979107/

Andrea Piacquadio. (2018, February 18). *A man in red shirt covering his face* [Image]. Pexels. https://www.pexels.com/photo/a-man-in-red-shirt-covering-his-face-3760043/

Andrea Piacquadio. (2020, February 25). *Woman in gray tank top while sitting on bed* [Image]. Pexels. https://www.pexels.com/photo/woman-in-gray-tank-top-while-sitting-on-bed-3807730/

Ashim D'Silva. (2016, July 19). *Black and white table lamp on brown wooden table* [Image]. Unsplash. https://unsplash.com/photos/3XvebFz_yhl

cottonbro studio. (2020, April 7). *Person in black pants and black shoes sitting on brown wooden chair* [Image]. Pexels. https://www.pexels.com/photo/person-in-black-pants-and-black-shoes-sitting-on-brown-wooden-chair-4101143/

Diva Plavalaguna. (2020, October 27). *Woman walking away from a man* [Image]. Pexels. https://www.pexels.com/photo/woman-walking-away-from-a-man-5711430/

Firmbee. (2015, February 3). *Office business accountant image* [Image]. Pixabay. https://pixabay.com/photos/office-business-accountant-620822/

Giulia Bertelli. (2016, May 20). *Woman wearing silver-colored ring* [Image]. Unsplash. https://unsplash.com/photos/dvXGnwnYweM

Juan Pablo Serrano Arena. (2018, March 20). *Man and woman sitting together in front of table* [Image]. Pexels. https://www.pexels.com/photo/man-and-woman-sitting-together-in-front-of-table-951290/

Karolina Grabowska. (2020, August 27). *A doctor and patient doing handshake* [Image]. Pexels. https://www.pexels.com/photo/a-doctor-and-patient-doing-handshake-5206923/

lilartsy. (2019, February 19). *Person holding on red pen while writing on book* [Image]. Unsplash. https://unsplash.com/photos/333oj7zFsdg

Liza Summer. (2020, December 31). *Unrecognizable woman demonstrating clothing in store* [Image]. Pexels. https://www.pexels.com/photo/unrecognizable-woman-demonstrating-clothes-in-store-6347535/

Liza Summer. (2021a, January 3). *Diverse women quarreling in room* [Image]. Pexels. https://www.pexels.com/photo/diverse-women-quarreling-in-room-6382675/

Liza Summer. (2021b, January 3). *Unrecognizable upset lady embracing knees sitting on chair* [Image]. Pexels. https://www.pexels.com/photo/unrecognizable-upset-lady-embracing-knees-sitting-on-chair-6382642/

paulbr75. (2018, February 5). *Red flag warning beach image* [Image]. Pixabay. https://pixabay.com/photos/red-flag-warning-beach-ocean-3132583/

Priscilla Du Preez. (2018, September 3). *Three women walking on brown wooden dock near high rise building during daytime* [Image]. Unsplash. https://unsplash.com/photos/mKJUoZPy70I

Timur Weber. (2021, June 30). *A couple talking while arguing* [Image]. Pexels. https://www.pexels.com/photo/a-couple-talking-while-arguing-8560383/

Towfiqu barbhuiya. (2022, April 15). *Red pouch on the table* [Image]. Pexels. https://www.pexels.com/photo/red-pouch-on-the-table-11826942/

Volodymyr Hryshchenko. (2019, December 17). *Shallow focus photo of white paper sheet mounted on cork board* [Image]. Unsplash. https://unsplash.com/photos/ZT9gjcJog6U

Yan Krukau. (2021, April 25). *Man in white dress shirt covering his face* [Image]. Pexels. https://www.pexels.com/photo/man-in-white-dress-shirt-covering-his-face-7640484/